BRI REECE

Catch & Cast

Reversing Negative Thinking Patterns

In59Seconds Publishing Co

Contents

Introduction

This book was written for anyone who has ever felt trapped inside their own mind, wondering why the pain seems to replay long after the moment that caused it has passed. It is for people who do not understand why a single thought can change their entire mood, derail their day, or reopen wounds they thought had healed. It is also for those who have never been told that thoughts are not commands and that just because a thought enters the mind does not mean it deserves to stay.

For many years, I believed I was at the mercy of my thoughts. When painful images from my past appeared, I assumed they were there for a reason and that I had no choice but to endure them. I did not understand that my suffering was being extended not by the original trauma, but by my continued focus on it. No one ever explained to me that awareness creates choice, and that choice creates freedom.

This book introduces a simple but life changing concept. You can catch a thought as it enters your mind, cast it out if it does not serve you, and replace it with a thought that supports your healing. This is not about pretending pain never happened. It is about refusing to relive it endlessly. It is about understanding that while pain may have been unavoidable, prolonged suffering is not.

Many people believe that controlling thoughts means denying emotion, suppressing feelings, or forcing positivity. That is not what this book teaches. Healing does not come from ignoring pain. It comes from acknowledging it and then choosing not to let it define your inner world forever. Negative thoughts do not make you weak or broken. They make you human. What matters is what you do once you become aware of them.

The method I share in this book is called Recognize, Reject, Replace. It is a system I developed through lived experience, trial, error, and deep self reflection. It helped me interrupt years of negative thinking patterns that were rooted in trauma, abandonment, and loss. It taught me that I could take responsibility for my inner life without blaming myself for what happened to me.

This book has been written with genuine love, care, and intention. My goal is not to judge you, criticize you, or suggest that you should have everything figured out by now. The truth is that every human being carries thought patterns, emotional wounds, fears, and beliefs that were formed through years of life experiences, and changing those patterns requires far more than willpower alone. It requires patience, self awareness, compassion, and a willingness to meet yourself with understanding rather than criticism. There will be moments throughout this journey when growth feels natural and encouraging, and there may be other moments when it feels uncomfortable because you are challenging ways of thinking that have existed within you for a very long time. If that happens, I want you to know that discomfort does not mean something is wrong. More often than not, it is a sign that meaningful change is taking place beneath the surface.

As you move through these pages, I encourage you to slow down and become an observer of your own inner world. Pay attention to the thoughts that repeatedly visit your mind, the emotions they create, and the stories you have been telling yourself for years without even realizing it. Notice which memories leave you feeling peaceful and empowered, and which ones continue pulling you back into pain, fear, resentment, or self doubt. This process is not about judging yourself for having certain thoughts. It is about becoming aware of them. Awareness is where every lasting transformation begins because once you can clearly see a pattern, you are no longer unconsciously controlled by it. The moment you recognize what is happening within your mind, you gain the ability to make different choices.

One of the greatest lessons I have learned throughout my own healing journey is that people often underestimate how much power they truly possess. Many have spent years believing they are trapped by their circumstances, controlled by their past, or destined to repeat the same emotional struggles forever. Nothing could be further from the truth. Healing is possible. Peace is possible. Emotional freedom is possible. A richer, healthier, and more fulfilling quality of life is possible. Your life was never meant to be defined exclusively by pain, disappointment, fear, or limitation. You were created to experience joy, connection, purpose, growth, and the deep sense of freedom that comes from understanding the incredible influence you have over your own thoughts, emotions, and perspective.

The pages ahead are designed to help you develop that understanding. Together, we will explore how to recognize the thoughts that quietly undermine your peace, identify the patterns that keep old wounds alive, and learn practical ways to release beliefs that no longer serve you. More importantly, you will discover how to intentionally replace those thoughts with perspectives that support your healing, strengthen your confidence, and align with the person you are becoming. My hope is that by the time you reach the final page, you will not only understand the process of catching and casting harmful thoughts, but also recognize that the power to create meaningful change has been within you all along.

1

The Mind Is Powerful, But It Is Not the Boss

Most people move through life believing that whatever shows up in their mind must be true, important, or worthy of attention. A thought appears, and without questioning it, they accept it. They assume it represents reality, memory, or instinct. Over time, this quiet acceptance becomes a habit, and that habit can slowly shape how a person feels about themselves, how they interpret the world, and how much peace they believe is available to them.

The mind is powerful, but power does not mean authority. Power simply means influence. The mind generates thoughts constantly, pulling from memory, emotion, fear, imagination, and experience. Many of those thoughts arrive automatically, without invitation. That does not mean they are instructions. It does not mean they are actual facts. It doesn't always mean they deserve your attention.

For many years, I did not know there was a difference between a thought and the truth. If an image entered my mind, I assumed it had meaning. If a painful memory resurfaced, I believed it was something I needed to sit with, analyze, or endure. No one ever explained to me that awareness creates space, and space creates choice. I lived as if my thoughts were in charge, when in reality, I had simply never questioned them.

The mind is designed to protect, but it does not always protect us accurately. We must train it. It holds onto past experiences as a way to prevent future pain, even when those experiences no longer apply. We have to train the mind to let those painful memories and images go. Trauma, abandonment, fear, and loss can shape the mind to replay certain images and stories long after the danger has passed. The intention may be safety, but the result is often suffering.

When a person believes the mind is the boss, they live re-actively. Their emotions rise and fall based on whatever thought happens to appear. A single memory can undo a good day. A single assumption can rewrite self worth. Over time, this creates exhaustion, anxiety, and a sense of powerlessness that feels permanent.

What most people have never been taught is that observation changes the relationship. When you take time to monitor your thoughts, only then can you change them. If you are too busy rushing around in life you may never notice how often you are thinking negatively. The moment you notice a thought instead of merging with it, something shifts. You move from being inside the thought to standing beside it. That is the beginning of freedom. The thought may still be there, but it no longer controls you by default. Most importantly, you realize you can change that thought.

This is not about fighting the mind or silencing it completely. That is neither realistic nor healthy. This is about understanding roles. The mind is a tool. It can assist, warn, remember, and imagine. But it was never meant to rule your emotional life without question. You were meant to participate consciously.

Many people fear that questioning their thoughts means denying their pain. That is not true. Pain deserves acknowledgment. Feelings deserve compassion. What does not deserve unlimited access is the repetition of suffering long after the moment has passed. There is a difference between honoring what happened and reliving it daily through unchecked thought patterns.

When you begin to understand that the mind is powerful but not the boss, you reclaim responsibility without blame. You stop seeing yourself as broken for having negative thoughts and start seeing yourself as capable of responding differently to them. This shift alone can bring relief, even before any technique is applied.

Throughout this book, you will learn how to develop that awareness and turn it into action. You will learn how to notice thoughts as they arrive, evaluate how they make you feel, and decide whether they belong in your inner world. This is not about perfection. It is about practice. It is about learning that you are not obligated to believe everything you think.

The mind is a non-judgmental garden. If you plant seeds of negativity and doubt that is exactly what will grow. On the other hand if you plant positive seeds, seeds of greatness, seeds of love, seeds of kindness then your garden will produce just that. So, it's truly all in your hands. This magic I speak of is non-bias. It won't tell you, "No, I refuse to produce this because it's not going to enhance your life." If you plant it, it will grow.

That analogy alone was enough for me to aggressively begin working on my M.I.N.D. techniques. I developed this acronym to help me remember the importance of the mind and maintaining a positive mental attitude.

MIND
M – Manipulating
I – Ideas in a
N – New
D – Direction

Learning to manipulate our ideas in a new direction was the main goal in writing this book. Yes! This helped me to control my mind's magic. If I was attending an event and I walked into the room feeling insecure because of recent weight gain, or maybe my skin wasn't at its best, instead of allowing the idea that other people in that room noticed my flaws to persist in my mind, I would change it to a different idea. I would say, "I am beautiful, people are staring at me because I look amazing today." Choosing to change my interpretation of others' glances changed my experience at the event, and as a result I enjoyed myself without allowing my mind to rob me of having a good time. We have no way of truly knowing what a person is thinking when they look our way, so why not choose to perceive the look as something coming from a positive place. Isn't that a more pleasant option.? Now, if I am concerned about an event I'm about to attend, I take a few minutes to meditate and visualize the exact way I want things to turn out. I create situations in my mind that make me feel loved. For example, I imagine everyone telling me how amazing I look and how gorgeous my dress is. In my mind, I create the entire day just as I desire it to be. If I want to be the center of attention, then I create that scenario in my mind. Taking the time to practice these imagination techniques makes it so much easier for me to enter the room. It's our world and we create our realities.

Learning how to catch a negative thought, cast it out and

replace the thought with a positive one that is more in line with what you desire, is the key to a happier life.

In the next chapter, we will talk about how pain becomes a pattern, and why the mind repeats certain images and stories long after the original experience has ended.

2

When Pain Turns Into a Pattern

Pain by itself is not what keeps people stuck. Pain happens in moments. It has a beginning, a middle, and an end, even when it is intense. What keeps people suffering is not the original experience, but the way the mind continues to revisit it long after the moment has passed. Pain turns into a pattern when the mind decides that replaying it is necessary, protective, or meaningful, even when it is no longer serving the person living with it.

The mind is excellent at remembering emotionally charged experiences. It stores them vividly, often attaching images, sounds, and sensations to those memories. When something reminds the mind of a past wound, it can bring the entire experience forward as if it is happening again. This is how a single moment can stretch itself across years. The body reacts. The emotions respond. The suffering feels current, even though the danger is not.

For a long time, I believed this repetition was unavoidable. When painful memories surfaced, I assumed they were there for a reason I needed to understand. I thought if I analyzed them enough, revisited them enough, or felt them deeply enough, they would eventually lose their power. What I did not realize was that each replay was reinforcing the pattern instead of dissolving it.

The mind does not distinguish between past and present the way we assume it does. When an image is replayed with emotional intensity, the nervous system responds as if the event is happening again. That is why people can feel exhausted, anxious, or defeated without anything currently going wrong. The suffering is being generated internally through repeated mental exposure.

This is especially true for people who have experienced trauma, abandonment, or sudden loss. The mind becomes hyper vigilant, scanning for threats and replaying memories in an attempt to stay prepared. The intention may be protection, but the outcome is constant emotional strain. Over time, this becomes familiar. Familiarity turns into habit. Habit turns into identity.

Many people begin to believe they are their pain because they have lived with it for so long. They introduce themselves to the world through their wounds, even when they desperately want to heal. This is not a failure of character. It is the result of an unchallenged mental pattern.

Pain often becomes a recurring pattern because the mind naturally returns to familiar thoughts, especially those carrying strong emotional weight. Over time, repeated thoughts begin creating well traveled pathways within the brain, making certain emotional responses feel almost automatic. A painful memory revisited often enough can start influencing the way a person interprets new experiences, relationships, opportunities, and even their sense of self. What began as a single difficult event can gradually evolve into an internal narrative that feels permanent simply because it has been rehearsed so many times. This is one of the reasons negative thinking can become so convincing. It is not evidence of weakness, failure, or a lack of character. More often, it reflects a mind that has become accustomed to traveling the same familiar roads again and again until those routes feel like the only ones available.

What makes this understanding so powerful is recognizing that the mind learned these patterns, which means the mind can also learn something different. The same process that strengthened those pathways can be used to create new ones. Awareness has a remarkable ability to interrupt patterns that once seemed impossible to change because the moment a person becomes conscious of what is happening internally, new choices become available. Every time a different perspective is considered, every time a healthier thought is chosen, and every time an old narrative is questioned rather than automatically accepted, something begins shifting beneath the surface. Change rarely happens all at once, but neither did the patterns that created the pain in the first place. Transformation often occurs through countless small moments of awareness that gradually accumulate until an entirely new way of thinking emerges.

When I first began understanding this, it completely changed the way I viewed healing. The conversation stopped being about what was wrong with me and started becoming about what had been practiced, reinforced, and repeated over time. That distinction matters because one perspective creates shame while the other creates possibility. If painful patterns were learned, then they can be unlearned. If limiting beliefs were adopted, then they can be challenged. If certain thoughts have been rehearsed for years, they do not have to remain permanent residents within the mind forever. There is something incredibly liberating about realizing that your history may have shaped you, but it does not have to define every chapter that follows.

Perhaps the greatest gift hidden within this understanding is hope. It reminds us that healing is not reserved for a select few fortunate people. Growth is not dependent upon perfection. Transformation does not require erasing the past or pretending painful experiences never happened. Real healing begins when we recognize that awareness gives us the power to respond differently, and every new response becomes an opportunity to create a different future than the one we may have unconsciously expected.

In the next chapter, we will explore one of the most misunderstood aspects of personal growth and emotional healing: the belief that having negative thoughts means something is wrong with you. As you will soon discover, the presence of difficult thoughts is not evidence of failure, weakness, or spiritual deficiency. Removing shame from the healing process is often the very thing that makes lasting transformation possible.

Negative Thinking Patterns

Discounting the Positive

"That doesn't count because.."

Should Statements

"I should always..."

Emotional Reasoning

"I feel... so it must be true"

Emotional Reasoning

"I feel... so it must be true."

All or Nothing

"If I'm not perfect, I'm a failure"

Catastrophizing

"What if everything goes wrong?"

3

You Are Not Broken for Having Negative Thoughts

One of the most damaging beliefs people carry is the idea that having negative thoughts means there is something wrong with them. This belief creates a second layer of suffering that is often more painful than the original thought itself. A thought appears, then shame follows. Judgment enters. Self criticism takes over. Before long, the person is not only dealing with the thought, but also with the belief that they are weak, flawed, or failing because the thought showed up at all.

Negative thoughts are part of being human. They are not evidence of failure. They are signals that the mind is responding to something it perceives as unfamiliar, unsafe, or unresolved. When people begin to judge themselves for having these thoughts, they unknowingly strengthen them. Shame gives negative thinking more power, not less.

For many years, I believed that if I were healed, faithful enough, or emotionally strong enough, these thoughts would stop completely. When they did not, I assumed I was doing something wrong. That belief kept me stuck far longer than the thoughts themselves. I was not only reliving pain, I was blaming myself for it.

What changed everything for me was understanding that thoughts do not define character. They do not determine worth. They do not measure progress. They are experiences passing through the mind, not declarations of truth. Once I separated my identity from my thoughts, I was finally able to work with them instead of against myself.

There is nothing shameful about noticing a painful thought. In fact, noticing it is the beginning of healing. Awareness means you are present. It means you are paying attention. It means you are no longer operating on autopilot. The goal is not to eliminate every negative thought. The goal is to change how you respond when one appears.

When people believe they should not be having certain thoughts, they often try to suppress them. Suppression rarely works. It usually leads to frustration and emotional tension. The mind pushes back harder when it feels controlled. What it responds to better is understanding, clarity, and direction.

Removing shame from the process allows healing to unfold naturally. You stop fighting yourself and start supporting yourself. Instead of asking why this keeps happening to you, you begin asking what this thought needs from you. Sometimes it needs to be acknowledged. Sometimes it needs to be released. Sometimes it simply needs to be replaced.

Negative thoughts do not make you ungrateful. They do not mean you lack faith. They do not cancel your growth. They simply indicate that the mind is still operating from old patterns that have not yet been interrupted. That does not make you broken. It makes you human and capable of change.

When you understand this, you stop fearing your own mind.

You stop bracing for thoughts as if they are enemies. You begin to see them as information. Information you can respond to with intention instead of fear.

Bad Thoughts
Good Thoughts

4

Mind Is All

One of the most important things we were never taught in school is that the mind controls our lives. We learned math, science, and history, but no one ever sat us down and explained that the quality of our thoughts determines the quality of our experience. When people hear that statement, they often feel confused. What does it really mean to say the mind controls our lives, and how is that different from the brain.

The brain and the mind are not the same thing, even though they work together. The brain is tangible. It can be studied, scanned, and dissected. Scientists have spent years examining the hemispheres and lobes of the brain and understanding how the nervous system communicates pain, sensation, and physical response. The mind, however, is not something you can cut open and study. It is intangible. You cannot see it, but you experience it constantly. It is the voice inside you that speaks, questions, remembers, imagines, and guides. In my belief, it is how God communicates with us. It is the origin of our individuality and the place where our soul expresses itself.

Human brains are built very similarly, but no two minds are

the same. Just like fingerprints, each mind carries its own patterns, perceptions, beliefs, and interpretations. This is why two people can experience the same situation and respond completely differently. The event may be the same, but the mind processing it is unique.

The mind is where choices are made. When someone makes you angry, there is no external signal telling you it is time to be angry. That decision happens internally. The same is true for kindness, generosity, and compassion. When you decide to help someone, give to someone, or comfort someone, that choice begins in the mind before it ever becomes an action. All of the most significant battles are negotiated internally before anything shows up on the outside.

Many people live reactively because they do not pause long enough to consult their mind consciously. They respond impulsively, allowing emotions to lead without awareness. Those reactions are not destiny. They are habits that can be interrupted. Anger and happiness both begin as choices in the mind. We can learn to guide those choices instead of letting them guide us.

Happiness does not begin in circumstances. It begins in the mind. Personal development does not start on the outside. It starts internally. This is why I say mind is all. Everything begins there. Health, peace, abundance, and fulfillment all have their roots in thought. Learning to manage and direct the mind is not optional if we want a better life. It is essential.

We think thousands of thoughts every single day. Counting them is not important, but monitoring them is. Thoughts are the missing piece in the creative process of life. If we do not pay attention to what we are thinking, we allow our mind to run unattended. Just like a child needs guidance to grow in a healthy direction, the mind needs direction to develop supportive patterns. If we do not guide it, it will guide us, often based on fear, past pain, or conditioning.

When we accept responsibility for the mind, everything changes. We stop feeling like life is happening to us and start realizing we are participating in it. We begin steering the ship instead of bracing for rough seas. We learn that we do not have to accept every thought, every image, or every emotional reaction as truth. We can intervene.

This understanding sets the foundation for everything that follows in this book. Once you know that the mind is powerful and that it shapes your life experiences, you are ready to learn how to work with it intentionally. This is where awareness becomes action. This is where Catch and Cast begins to take form, not as a concept, but as a daily practice.

MIND IS ALL

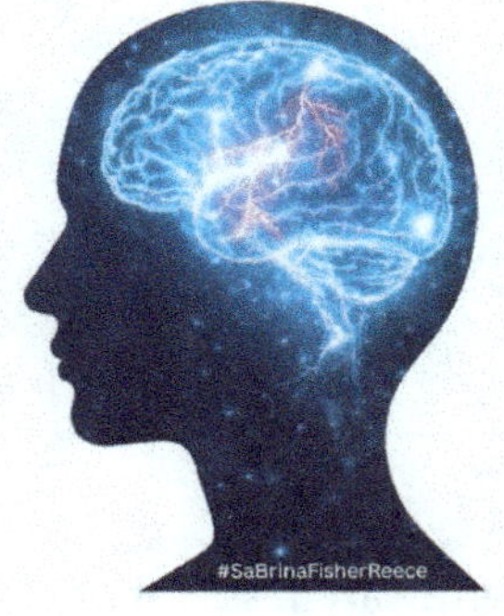

MIND =

M = Manipulate

I = Ideas in a

N = New

D = Direction

5

Catch and Cast

There comes a moment in this work when awareness stops being passive and becomes active. You are no longer just noticing thoughts as they arrive. You are engaging with them. This is where Catch and Cast becomes real. Catching a thought means you are present enough to intercept it before it settles in and takes root. Casting it means you are no longer willing to let it occupy space in your mind simply because it showed up.

For a long time, I believed that once a thought entered my mind, I was obligated to entertain it. I assumed it needed to be analyzed, understood, or endured. That belief kept me stuck in cycles of pain that felt endless. What I eventually learned is that thoughts are like visitors. Some are welcome and very supportive. Others arrive uninvited can be disruptive. Just because they knock does not mean they deserve entry.

Catching a thought requires presence. It happens in real time. A familiar image surfaces. A familiar story begins to play. Instead of letting it run, you pause. You notice it. You feel how it affects your body and emotions. That pause is powerful. It interrupts the automatic response that once felt unavoidable. It gives you back your authority.

Casting a thought is a conscious decision. It is not denial. It is discernment. You are not pretending the thought never appeared. You are acknowledging it and deciding it does not belong. This choice may feel uncomfortable at first, especially if the thought has been repeated for years. Familiarity can create attachment, even when the thought causes pain. Letting it go can feel strange, like stepping away from something known.

Many people fear that casting out a thought means suppressing emotion. That is not what this is. Emotions deserve to be felt. What does not deserve unlimited access is the mental replay that keeps reopening wounds. Catch and Cast allows you to honor your feelings without reliving the trauma that created them.

When I began practicing this, I realized how often my suffering was being extended by unchallenged thoughts. Memories of abandonment. Images of loss. Beliefs about worthiness that were never true. Catching those thoughts gave me the opportunity to stop them at the door. Casting them out created space for something new.

This process takes patience. At first, thoughts may feel fast and overwhelming. You may miss them. You may catch them after they have already done damage. That does not mean you are failing. It means you are learning. Each moment of awareness strengthens your ability to intervene earlier the next time.

Catch and Cast is not about control through force. It is about choice through your own conscious awareness. You are learning to decide what deserves your attention and what does not. You are learning that your mind does not have to be a place where every thought is entertained equally. It can be a place of intention.

This chapter prepares you for the deeper work ahead. Catch and Cast is the doorway to taking control of your thoughts. In the next few chapters, we will move fully into the Recognize, Reject, Replace system and begin applying this practice in a structured, repeatable way that can change how you experience your inner world every day.

#CatchAndCast

6

Awareness Is the Turning Point

Nothing changes until something is noticed. That may sound simple, but it is one of the most overlooked truths when it comes to healing the mind. For years, I lived inside my thoughts without realizing I was inside them. I was reacting, remembering, replaying, and believing without ever pausing long enough to observe what was actually happening internally. Awareness was not something I practiced. It was something I stumbled into, and once I did, everything began to shift.

Awareness is the moment you realize that a thought has entered your mind and you are still present enough to respond to it. It is not judgment. It is not criticism. It is not control. It is simply noticing. Most people move so quickly through life that they never give themselves the space to listen to what they are thinking. They wake up, rush through their day, and fall into bed exhausted, never realizing how much of their emotional energy was spent responding to unexamined thoughts.

When I began slowing down, even slightly, I started to hear the internal dialogue that had been running my life. I noticed patterns. I noticed repetition. I noticed how certain thoughts made my body tense and my heart feel heavy. I also noticed that those thoughts often had nothing to do with the present moment. They were echoes from the past that had been given unlimited access to my now.

Awareness does not require hours of meditation or isolation from the world. It begins in ordinary moments that most people overlook. It appears in the brief pause before a reaction. It shows up when you notice your mood change and become curious about what triggered it. Sometimes it arrives when a familiar feeling of heaviness settles in and you decide to trace it back to the thought, image, or belief that quietly surfaced beneath the surface of your attention. These moments seem small while they are happening, yet they hold tremendous power because they interrupt patterns that have often been running unnoticed for years.

This is where many people misunderstand the work. They assume awareness means they are failing. They believe that noticing a negative thought is evidence that something is wrong with them or that they have not made enough progress. In reality, the opposite is true. Awareness is not proof of failure. It is proof that change is already beginning. You cannot change what remains hidden from you. You cannot redirect a pattern you have never learned to recognize. The simple act of noticing is what opens the door to every other possibility. It is the moment where unconscious repetition gives way to conscious choice.

Once awareness enters the picture, the mind begins to lose its automatic authority. Thoughts no longer move through you unquestioned. They no longer get to dictate your emotional state without your participation. Instead of being swept away by every mental current, you step back and observe it. You become the witness rather than the passenger. That distance may seem subtle, but it changes everything. A thought can only control you when it goes unexamined. The moment you see it clearly, you gain the ability to decide whether it deserves your energy, your attention, or your belief.

For me, awareness was the first real sign that I was no longer powerless. Before that, I thought my thoughts were simply happening to me. I believed the fear, the doubt, the worry, and the negativity were forces I had no control over. Then I began to notice how often I was feeding those thoughts with my own attention. I was replaying them, entertaining them, and allowing them to take up space in my mind long after they first appeared.

That realization could have made me feel guilty, but it did not. What I felt was relief. For the first time, I understood that I was not trapped inside a process I could not influence. If I had been participating in my own suffering, then I also had the ability to participate in my own healing. If I had the power to repeatedly reinforce negative thoughts, then I also had the power to interrupt them. The same mind that had been rehearsing fear could begin rehearsing possibility. The same attention that had been strengthening doubt could begin strengthening belief. Awareness showed me that I was not a victim of my thinking. I was an active participant in it, and that meant I could choose a different direction.

Awareness is very gentle. It does not force change or demand perfection from you. It simply creates the space you need to take control of your mind. Within that space, you can meet yourself honestly without judgment or shame. You can observe what is happening without immediately and impulsively trying to fix it. Awareness reminds you that you are not broken because certain thoughts appear in your mind. You are becoming conscious of patterns that were previously operating in the background. That is growth, even when it feels uncomfortable.

As awareness eventually becomes a habit, everything else starts to become possible. The choices that once seemed unavailable begin to appear. Your sudden reactions become intentional responses. Old patterns become visible enough to challenge. This is where Catch and Cast moves from an interesting idea into a daily practice. You cannot catch a thought you never notice or recognized. You cannot cast out a pattern you remain unaware of. Awareness is the foundation beneath every step of this process. Without it, nothing changes. With it, change becomes possible.

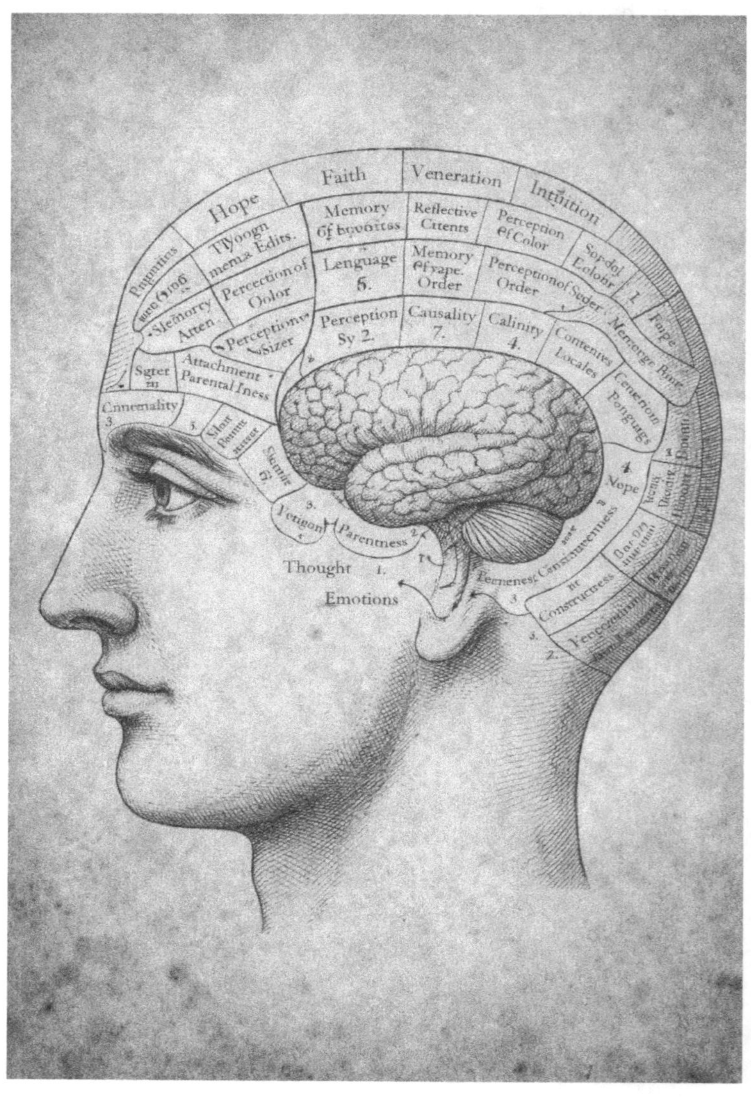

7

Imagine the Best

In order to have the best you must think that way. You must think that "The Best" is possible and believe that you deserve it.The imagination is a great way to develop that mindset. The imagination is a magnificent tool. I consider the imagination a gift from God. We must see something in our mind long before it ever shows up in our lives. Learning to think positively allows us to sharpen our imagination. If you stop for a second and reflect, you will notice that many of the thoughts you focus on have also been creating a mental picture in our mind. You have been imagining it. Now this is great if the images you are using your imagination to create are good ones. If the things you are planting in our minds are wonderful things that bring you happiness and joy then you have nothing to worry about. You are headed down the right road. However once you actually take the time to dissect your thoughts you will notice that you imagine not only good things, but horrible things as well. We all spend a lot of time thinking about the things we do not want to happen in our lives. The things that we are afraid of also seep into our imagination as well. These are the thoughts we want to convert into positive ones. Instead of thinking you will never find love. Convert that into a beautiful thought, maybe an image of you and your new mate, madly in love on an amazing tropical vacation. Instead of believing your business will fail. Create a mental image of you at your business's 15 year anniversary party. Picture all your friends and family surrounding you, celebrating you and wishing you 15 more years in business.

I wrote this particular book to teach you how to cast out the negative thoughts and keep the positive thoughts as the predominant thoughts. You create your reality with the thoughts you hold in your mind. Don't be upset with yourself for having negative thoughts. On the contrary, be pleased with yourself for being able to recognize them. Only when you acknowledge their existence, can you change them. Having the thought is not the problem but allowing your mind to stay focused on the bad thought is. Having a fleeting negative thought is less of a concern than allowing your mind to stay focused on that thought. Think it, realize it is negative and then stop your mind in its tracks and replace that thought with a positive one.

When I speak motivationally I teach the **"Catch and Cast and Recognize, Reject, Replace"** concept. It is also the title of Chapter nine in my second book *"Your Mind Is Magic."* Recognizing negative thoughts is the first step. Making a conscious choice to reject those thoughts is the second step. Replacing the negative thoughts with positive ones is the final step. Master this concept and it will change your life.

We create bad imaginary situations in our head and actually suffer the emotions associated with them. For example, one day my two youngest daughters and I were driving down the street coming from shopping. My 10 year old said she needed to do her homework in Google Docs. Since I use Google Docs to create my books. I replied "Please make sure you create your own account because I don't need anything going wrong with my books." She is known for changing passwords and creating accounts she can't remember how to get back into. I began to get angry at the idea of her accidentally getting into my google docs account and deleting some of my work. The entire rest of the ride home I felt myself getting more and more mad. I had to remind myself that this situation did not happen. The simple idea of it had me livid. Which caused me unnecessary suffering at that moment. I literally had to internally say to myself "She didn't do it yet SaBrina, this didn't happen". This is that self check tool I speak of often in this book. Her simply mentioning Google Docs made me create that entire hypothetical situation in my mind and actually get mad about it. Which caused a physical reaction from my body, for something that never actually took place. Many of us do this from time to time. We invent drama in our own heads and mentally and physically react to it as if it is a reality.

We imagine things and literally allow ourselves to generate the same emotions as if it actually happened. This is unnecessary mental anguish. This pointless suffering can be avoided. This is creating hell on earth in that moment for ourselves. Here I am riding home mad at my 10 year old for something that never happened. I believe if we don't stop negative thinking such as this in its tracks then we will manifest that exact imaginary situation. If we keep imagining something terrible happening, eventually it will. Self regulation is a key component in mastering positive thinking. We suffer through so many harmful, hurtful situations in our mind that may never actually happen. Let's save those emotions for real life circumstances.

Our imagination is a gift. Let's use that gift to enhance our lives, not cause ourselves more pain and strife. Life can be a wonderful experience once we eliminate unnecessary suffering. I know most humans believe that they have no control over what happens in their lives but this is simply untrue. The Divine Creator of us all, whom I choose to call God, gave us control over our lives. We were given free will. This allows us the ability to create. No we can't control everything but we can learn to control how we think and our thoughts are a vital key to the situations and circumstances that show up in our lives. Having a better life experience depends greatly upon the thoughts we choose to focus on. This book's purpose is to teach you the importance of controlling your thought patterns and making sure the predominant thoughts are positive.

Suffering is not always caused by us but in many instances we allow other people to cause us unnecessary pain. For example in September of 2023 I received the 2 Citation from the City of Los Angeles for parking my H2 Hummer on my grass. I have owned this property since 2000 and I simply don't drive the big tank anymore. I didn't want to sell it because I purchased it in 2003 when Hummers first came out at the full price of $85,000. Even though it was inoperable due to sitting on my front lawn for 6 years straight. I still was undecided about selling it. Many people had knocked on my front door over the years offering to buy it. I always said "Nope I'm gonna fix it up one day". Well that day never came and heading into the 7th year of it, sitting there with dry rotted tires and a kill switch that I didn't know how to turn back on, I still wasn't ready to sell it. Parting with it was not yet an option.

I began to get citations from the city of Los Angeles. After conversing with a neighbor who planted the idea in my head that another neighbor was the culprit who had actually called the city of Los Angeles to complain, I got mad. I didn't know which noisy neighbor made the phone call or if it was even true, but I accepted it as fact and developed an attitude about it. I scanned the street daily with my eyes shooting negative beams of bad energy to the neighbor or neighbors I felt were capable of causing me this unnecessary expense. Up until this point I had never had any problems with my neighbors for the entire 23 years I lived there. They were all much older than me and looked out for me like parents. The point to this is for however long I waged a mental and emotional war on the suspected neighbor only I was suffering. I was causing myself emotional distress. They had no idea I was mad and possibly not even one of them called the city. Maybe the City inspector was just driving by and stopped. He could have noticed the truck sitting on the grass with two flat tires himself. Maybe there is a law that says you can't park a car on your grass for 6 years. Who knows, but I caused myself to have an internal battle which provoked harsh feelings about others for no darn reason. I made a choice to suffer inside every time I got mad. Every time I screamed to myself "This is my property, they need to mind their own business." I was suffering inside and allowing negative feelings that did not serve me well. To this day not one of my neighbors knows about this all out war I waged on them because it all happened inside of me. I was fighting the battle from the north, south, east and west all on my own. If I saw one of them outside in their yard I waved and said "Good Morning as usual." They were none the wiser. I have to laugh at this because many of us do this. So many times we harbor ill feelings with misinformation. If we want peace internally we must learn to identify and stop this behavior. The thoughts we hold in our mind need to align with the desired outcome. We should take a moment and intentionally imagine the positive relationships we want to have with others. Imagine the ideal outcome of a challenging situation. For Example, I could take a few minutes, close my eyes and imagine receiving a letter from the City inspector saying that the fees for parking my truck on my grass have been waived. Remember "All Things Are Possible," so don't allow your logical mind to talk you out of things. Don't think about the bad that can happen. I understand that retraining your mind takes focus and a lot of conscious mental action but it will be beneficial in the long run. The imagination is a beautiful gift from the creator that allows us to create a life of love, peace, happiness, great health and abundance. If you can Imagine it you can have it. Try to commit to a few moments a day to sit alone quietly and purposefully imagine the life you desire. Imagine the best, not the worst. Imagine good not bad. Imagine happiness not sadness. Imagine wealth not poverty and do it so regularly that it becomes a habit. This is how we change our lives for the better.

Miracles

We say we believe in miracles. However when they actually happen the logical brain instantly tries to dismiss the fact that it is simply a miracle. One day in 2023 my daughters and I were driving down Slauson Ave in Los Angeles Ca and all the traffic lights were out. We came to an intersection that had become infamous due to a horrible accident which resulted in the death of six people there a year prior. The incident involved a traveling nurse named Nicole Linton. She was the driver of the vehicle that killed six people in the intersection in August of 2022. As I got closer to the intersection I began to feel a little anxiety due to the intersection's deathly history and because all lights were out. The traffic lights had failed from the north, south, east and west. Although most people know the rules of the road and to implement stop and go when lights are out. Some people simply don't adhere to that. I was beginning to get nervous. I was two cars away from being the next car to cross the intersection and I began to pray aloud. "Lord, please keep us covered and protected with your blood. Please make sure everyone makes it through the intersection safely." Mid prayer and right before I was next to cross the intersection. All the street lights miraculously popped back on. This happened while I was still praying before the street police had a chance to arrive to direct traffic safely. The lights just came on by themselves. Instantly it was my car's turn to cross the intersection. WOW! I looked at my daughter in disbelief. I said, "Oh My God." Once again we had been a witness to another miracle that very well could have saved lives. I started telling my kids about the power of prayer and how miracles are real. They have heard it all before but it is amazing to see small miracles happen in real time. I don't particularly like driving much anyway. I don't feel I'm very good at it and I experience a lot of anxiety when I drive. This is an area where I have to commit a lot of time to making sure I'm not driving around town with bad thoughts. Particularly thoughts of fear. I can not even for one minute allow myself to entertain continuous thoughts of getting hit by another car or dying in some horrible car accident. However this has been a challenge for me. I began to notice once I got into my early 50's I was consumed with my fear of driving. I had to drive for necessity of course but I did not enjoy it. I had two beautiful completely paid off luxury vehicles but still didn't want to drive. In regards to finding some positives in the Nicole Linton tragedy. I think that deathly catastrophe made many people drive safer. It's truly unfortunate that so many people died. One of which was an infant child. It truly rocked the city to its core. However if indeed it makes some speed demons slow down and consider others while driving then that is some positive drawn from it. Many lives may be saved just from people being more conscious while driving.

One day in April 2023 I was driving with my daughters to an appointment. I had recently been talking to them about when they become drivers even though the light turns green they should not speed right out. I told them to always pause for a moment and of course look both ways before proceeding into the intersection. I was telling them that quite often there is someone trying to speed through the light before it turns red so they should always pause even after the light is visibly green. On this particular day It was raining off and on. I made a left onto a street called El Segundo blvd. Shortly after turning we came to a red light. Once it turned green I did exactly what I taught my kids to do. I paused, I looked right and then left and proceeded to drive forward into the intersection. Suddenly on my left side I saw a car flying toward me at an unbelievable speed. It was traveling so fast that I could see the water from the wet street kicking up all around the tires of the car. I screamed, turned my head forward quickly and pressed the gas pedal with my right foot attempting to accelerate and avoid being crashed into by the speeding car. As soon as I pressed the gas to accelerate I instantly glanced up into the rear view mirror I saw a cloud of smoke. Somehow the car missed us. I believed then and still believe now that a miracle happened that day. I was able to clearly see the car on my driver's side meaning it was already that close to me. I don't believe any amount of acceleration could have caused us to avoid being hit. Even if the sudden gas pedal push advanced us a few inches it wouldn't have been enough to push past the length of my long 2011 CLS 550. At the very least the back of my car would have been hit. If anyones knows how long the body is of that particular make and model you will understand what I am saying. It still would caught the tall end of the car no matter how fast I tried to speed up. But it didn't. My 10 year old daughter Journey was in the back seat. We were not hit at all. It somehow completely missed us. The logical human me is saying "Impossible." The spiritual me is accepting the obvious miracle that saved me and my two daughters that day. Although the creator gave us free will and control over our own lives. It's clear to me now that there are times when God, the divine source intervenes. It's so difficult for the logical brain to accept that. I went over and over it in my head. There is no possible way our car was not hit that day other than the amazing grace and mercy of God. I will forever be grateful

8

Recognize, Reject, Replace

The most effective tool I have ever used to interrupt negative thinking patterns is learning how to catch a thought as it is coming in and making a conscious decision to cast it right back out. This process did not come from theory or study. It came from necessity. I could not change what was happening in my life until I became honest about what was happening in my mind. Negative thinking patterns cannot be changed if they are not first recognized. That recognition requires stillness. It requires slowing down long enough to listen to what you are actually thinking instead of moving through life on autopilot.

Recognizing that you are actively participating in negative thinking is a turning point. Many people spend years completely unaware that most of the thoughts they allow to circulate in their minds are not supportive. They are fear based, self critical, or rooted in past pain. Humanity as a whole underestimates the power of thought and its impact on quality of life. Mind is all, and thoughts are everything. Every outcome begins with a single thought. God gave us the ability to create meaningful, fulfilling lives, but that creation always begins internally.

It is essential to monitor your thoughts. Think of your thoughts as seeds and your mind as a garden. The garden will always produce what is planted. If you plant thoughts of fear, illness, lack, or unworthiness, that is exactly what will grow. This is not punishment. It is cause and effect. Once I understood this, I realized that my inner world required just as much care and intention as anything I wanted to grow on the outside.

At first, learning to observe thoughts can feel challenging. Many people are surprised by how often negative thoughts appear. This does not mean you are doing something wrong. It means you are becoming aware. Anything practiced consistently becomes a habit, and awareness is a habit worth developing. This is why I created the Recognize, Reject, Replace system. It gave me a clear way to respond instead of react.

Recognize is the first step, and it requires slowing down. Life moves fast, and most people rush from one obligation to the next without ever checking in with themselves. Creating moments throughout the day to notice what thoughts you are allowing into your mind is necessary. Even more important is noticing which thoughts you allow to linger. Recognition does not exist to make you feel bad. If the word negative feels uncomfortable, you do not need to use it. What matters is learning to distinguish between thoughts that support you and thoughts that harm you. Once that distinction is clear, change becomes possible.

Reject is the moment you realize you have a choice. Many people live most of their lives without knowing they can reject a thought. They assume every thought that enters their mind must be accepted. This is not true. You have the ability to refuse thoughts that make you feel afraid, ashamed, guilty, or defeated. The way a thought makes you feel is your first indicator. If it consistently produces pain, it does not belong. Once a thought has been identified and labeled, it becomes easier to recognize when it returns. You no longer allow it to take over simply because it is familiar.

Replace is where your power becomes active. Once space has been created by rejecting a harmful thought, you get to decide what fills that space. This is not about lying to yourself. It is about choosing intentionally. Fear can be replaced with courage. Defeat can be replaced with resilience. Self hatred can be replaced with truth. This is how you become the master of your inner world. This is where healing begins to feel possible.

When I first began this work, I was vulnerable. The desire to heal can make people susceptible to giving their power away. I trusted individuals who claimed they could heal me, only to learn that no one else holds that authority. I had not yet realized that God had already placed within me everything I needed. Giving someone else control over my healing delayed my progress and caused unnecessary pain. That experience taught me a powerful lesson. Guidance can help, but responsibility always belongs to the individual.

Witnessing the traumatic loss of my grandmother at a young age shaped my thinking in ways I did not understand for many years. The memories replayed themselves without permission. I believed I was powerless against them. What I later learned is that those images did not need to be revisited endlessly for healing to occur. Healing required interruption, choice, and compassion toward myself.

I also learned that unmet emotional needs can cause us to seek validation in unhealthy ways. When love is missing early in life, people often look for it externally, believing someone else can fix what feels broken. That belief creates attachment and disappointment. Forgiveness became essential to my healing, not because others were perfect, but because I deserved peace.

"Father forgive them for they know not what they do," Luke 23:34

Forgiveness does not mean excusing harm. It means choosing not to carry the weight of it forever. Learning to love myself required releasing expectations that others could make me whole. True healing began when I turned inward and accepted responsibility for my emotional growth.

I now understand that I had been reinforcing my own suffering through repeated thoughts about abandonment and worthlessness. No one was reminding me daily of those experiences. I was doing that myself. Once I recognized the pattern, rejected the lie, and replaced it with truth, everything changed. I reminded myself that I am a creation of God with purpose, value, and limitless potential.

We are all worthy of total and complete happiness. Painful experiences do not change that. Negative thoughts do not define who you are. They are habits that can be changed but first we must Recognize them. Reject the thoughts that harms you. Replace it with what heals you. This practice has the power to change your life, just as it changed mine.

1
Step 1
Recognize
Recognize the negative thought
as it enters your mind
2
Step 2
Reject
Make a conscious choice
to reject the thought
3
Step 3
Replace
Replace the thought with
uplifting, powerful thoughts it
make you feel good abut yourself
4

9

Why Healing Can Make You Vulnerable

There is a stage in healing that is rarely talked about, and it is one of the most delicate. When you finally decide that you want peace, when you become committed to changing how you think and feel, you can become emotionally open in ways you are not prepared for. That openness can feel like hope, relief, and eagerness, but it can also leave you vulnerable if you do not yet fully understand your own power.

When someone is hurting deeply, the desire to be free from that pain can be overwhelming. In that state, it is easy to believe that someone else holds the answers you have been searching so long for. I know this because I have most definitely lived it. I believed that if I found the right teacher, the right guide, or the right method, my pain would finally disappear. I did not yet realize that healing is not something that can be handed to you. It is something you must participate in consciously. No human being can heal you. You must take the reigns yourself and make it the most important task you must complete. it is detrimental to the quality of your life.

During my own healing journey, there was a season of my life

47

when I placed my trust in someone who appeared to embody everything I hoped to become. He was handsome, charismatic, and carried himself with a quiet confidence that seemed to radiate certainty. We attended the same spiritual center, and he taught meditation classes that I occasionally joined. Whenever he spoke, people listened. His words carried the kind of conviction that makes you believe he has discovered something you have not yet found. At the time, I was carrying wounds that had followed me for years. Trauma had shaped the way I saw myself, the way I experienced relationships, and the way I moved through the world. More than anything, I wanted relief from the constant weight of it. I wanted peace and freedom. I wanted to believe that somewhere ahead of me there was an end to the mental and emotional struggle I had known for so long.

Looking back now, I can see that my vulnerability had very little to do with a lack of intelligence and everything to do with a deep longing to heal. When someone is hurting, hope becomes incredibly powerful. Hope can inspire remarkable change, but it can also make us overlook things we would normally question. Every encouraging word feels significant when it may not be. Every promise of healing feels like a long awaited lifeline. Every person who appears certain can begin to look like someone who possesses answers we cannot yet find within ourselves. I wanted this mans words to be true because I needed them to be true. The possibility that someone had finally discovered the path out of suffering was far more appealing than the difficult reality that healing would require me to walk that path myself.

What I did not understand then was that I was repeating the very pattern I needed to break. Although I believed I was moving toward healing, I was still placing my power outside of myself and solely in this man's ability to heal me. Instead of trusting my own awareness, I was looking to someone else for certainty. Instead of listening to my intuition, I was measuring my experiences against another person's authority. Even when moments arose that did not sit right with me, even when something deep inside whispered that I should pay closer attention, I found ways to dismiss those feelings. The desire to heal can become so strong that it convinces us to negotiate with our own instincts. Pain has a way of clouding judgment when relief feels close enough to touch.

One of the hardest truths I have learned is that desperation often disguises itself as faith. From the outside, the two can look remarkably similar. Both involve hope. Both involve belief. Both require openness. Yet one is rooted in trust while the other is rooted in fear. Desperation whispers that someone else must have what you are missing. It convinces you that your answers exist somewhere outside of you, waiting to be handed over by the right teacher, the right program, the right relationship, or the right spiritual guide. Faith, on the other hand, understands that support may come from many places, but the deepest source of healing can never be transferred from one person to another.

This experience taught me a lesson that was painful but necessary. No human being has the ability to heal another person completely. Guidance can be valuable. Wisdom can be helpful. Teachers, mentors, therapists, and spiritual leaders can all play meaningful roles in someone's growth. Yet no matter how knowledgeable they may be, none of them can do your healing for you. The responsibility always returns to the individual. Anyone who presents themselves as the answer rather than a guide should be approached with caution. Genuine wisdom does not encourage dependence. Genuine wisdom encourages self trust. It points you back to your own awareness rather than demanding that you surrender it.

As I continued my journey, I began to understand that discernment is just as important as vulnerability. Opening your heart is necessary for healing, but keeping your awareness active is equally important. Healing does not require blind trust in others. It requires conscious trust. There is a difference between the two. One asks you to ignore what feels wrong in order to preserve hope. The other allows hope and wisdom to exist together. Real growth happens when you remain connected to yourself even while receiving guidance from others.

This reflection is not rooted in blame, bitterness, or regret. It comes from my learned awareness. Countless people find themselves in similar situations while searching for healing. Some place their trust in charismatic teachers. Others place it in relationships, belief systems, or promises that seem to offer an escape from pain. That does not make them foolish. It makes them human beings. Sometimes suffering creates a longing for relief, and that longing can sometimes lead us down paths that teach difficult lessons. What matters is not that we made mistakes along the way. What matters is whether we learn from them and reclaim the parts of ourselves we unknowingly handed away.

The most important realization I carried forward from that experience was understanding that everything I had been searching for already existed within me. The peace I wanted was not locked inside another person. The answers I sought were not hidden behind someone else's approval. God had never placed my healing in another human being's hands. He had placed it within my awareness, my ability to choose, my willingness to observe my thoughts, and my capacity to return to truth when I wandered away from it. The more deeply I understood this, the less I felt compelled to search for someone to save me.

That is why vulnerability is not weakness. Vulnerability is simply a stage of the journey that many of us need to go through. It is often the doorway through which true healing begins. When it is paired with wisdom and awareness, it becomes one of the greatest strengths a person can develop. You learn how to receive support without surrendering your power. You learn how to listen without abandoning your own voice. You learn how to respect guidance without placing anyone on a pedestal. Most importantly, you fully understand that true healing is not about finding someone to rescue you. It is about remembering the strength, wisdom, and connection to God that have been within you all along.

10

Subconscious Re-Programming Made Simple

I know this may sound complicated. What the heck is subconscious reprogramming? Even better, what is a subconscious? That is definitely a question most will ask. I sure did.

Learning the definition of the subconscious and the difference between the subconscious and the conscious minds helped me to fully understand how important my thoughts were. It gave me a better understanding of the importance of the mind and what we allow into it. From as young as infants our subconscious is being shaped.

Our belief system begins to form and assign judgment to people, places and things. For example, if we are spanked as a young child for talking too much. We form the subconscious belief that talking too much is bad and we will be punished for it. Thus, we make a conscious effort throughout our lives to minimize our words.

Some of us were warned by our parents and grandparents to "beware" of sickness and disease, because many in our family had died before us of specific diseases that were believed to run in the family. Subconsciously we fear becoming sick and dying of these diseases. These fears are ingrained with-in us and most of us don't even realize we have them.

I had studied so many scientists and authors who specialize in the subconscious mind and the general consensus amongst them is that our inner world affects our outer world. So many of the descendants before us knew this fact. Why weren't we taught this from birth? If our subconscious is so critical to our emotional advancement, why isn't this information taught as early as preschool? As irritated as I was that I did not know this information early in life, I am equally as grateful that I acquired it before I died.

For years, I believed my mother who had abandoned me as a baby could heal me if she would just call and apologize for allowing drugs to consume her life. Her negative choices prevented her from being capable of being a good mother to me and my five siblings. I spent years feeling unworthy and unwanted because of her choice to abandon and abuse her children. The story I was told of her putting me into a suitcase as a three-month-old baby and closing it, leaving me for dead, haunted me for years. Knowing this fact caused me to grow up with severe self-worth issues and random bouts of depression. Her actions caused me to form the subconscious belief that I was not valuable and worthy of life. I formed the belief that if my own mother did not see value in me then no one would. This is the very belief that I would need to reprogram. Learning that this was necessary and taking the steps to reprogram that belief was half the battle won. Unfortunately, I did not begin that process until I was forty years old. I am open and transparent in my books so others can begin the healing process sooner than I did.

Throughout my life I never once remember someone approaching me and reminding me that I was unwanted by my own mother, not once. Most of the people in my life during my twenties and thirties had no idea about my past. The only time I heard that horrible story of abandonment was when I told it to myself. Inside I would say, "SaBrina, you don't deserve love because your mother didn't love you." I was the only one guilty of that. I also chose to take my mother's actions personally. She was an addict who doesn't even remember most of the horrible things she did. In no way am I excusing her behavior, but I am pointing out how we can carry hurt and pain for so many years from people who are not sharing that weight. We are the only ones suffering, and internal suffering is damaging to our mental and physical health. Suffering is a choice we do not have to make. After studying Don Miguel Ruiz's concepts on not taking things personally in "The Four Agreements," I slowly began to change my perception of her actions. Her actions were more about her and her own mental darkness than they were about me. This helped me to slowly develop self worth. No one deserves to travel through life feeling like they do not matter, especially when those feelings are provoked by the actions of other human beings.

On June 18, 2018, my biological mother died. I did not know how to feel. For years, I would always say that I couldn't care less if she died, so I didn't expect to feel anything when I received the news of her death. On the contrary, I was suddenly struck with crippling pain. I felt it engulf me from the ground up and I could not stop it nor did I understand why it was there. I didn't love her. I didn't even know her. Because of her drug addiction I was never given the opportunity to love her. She definitely didn't love me. So why was I in pain?

Now in tears, I became angry that I was hurting. I thought to myself who hurts and sheds tears for a mother that never loved them? Who hurts for a mother that tried to kill them? What the heck is wrong with me? Why am I crying? I was mad and stuck in one place. I literally could not move. This unwanted emotion consumed me. I don't remember who I called first or how I finally moved from that position, but I did make a few phone calls. It felt unusual because all those in my life that were close to me knew that I did not have a relationship with my mother. I recall a friend telling me that what I was experiencing was called DNA pain. I didn't want it and I was resentful that it appeared even in death that my mother still had some emotional hold over me. I vowed at that moment that I would not be attending the funeral.

As the days went by, I learned about even more unacceptable abusive things my mother had done and had not made amends for. I was angry and I was happy she was dead. I began to feel grateful that I was not aware of all of the hurt and devastation she had caused our family. I was certain that God had intervened and protected me from all the facts because I most certainly would have felt compelled to confront her and force her to rectify her wrong doings. I began to feel that I had been spared from knowing exactly how evil she was. I understand to some that may sound harsh, but I have to be completely transparent in order for you to understand the dark state of mind I had to heal from.

Those feelings of gratitude were short-lived, and eventually I began to get depressed, which infuriated me. Thoughts of suicide and unworthiness returned. I had not been depressed in years. I had done so much emotional work over the years and I could not believe that this death was erasing all of that. I can only assume that there must have been a deep secret part of me that held out hope that she would finally lick all of our mental and emotional wounds and heal all of our hearts one day. I was wrong. After finding out that my mother had been in hospice care for months and was aware that she was dying, yet didn't reach out to her six children to apologize for her abandonment and abusive behavior. I was devastated all over again. I felt like all the work I had done to heal myself had been wasted.

I am not exactly sure what changed. I have no idea why I suddenly woke up one day and decided to speak at my mother's funeral. It must have been God, but I woke up one morning and decided I needed to participate in her funeral. I began communicating with my older sister and helped to arrange an obituary that was a little more honest than the one that had originally been created by my younger sister. The first line of her version of the obituary said "Shirley Ann Tillman was a great mother." What? "Are you kidding me," I thought. "Why would you write something that is a complete lie." I was not trying to be mean, but why would we ever say that she was a great mother in her obituary? She allowed me to create a more realistic version of the obituary. It wasn't my goal to bash my mother, I simply wanted to get this process over with so I could move on with my life, especially since I felt her death was putting me back at square one emotionally. I contacted some of her living relatives from Texas and asked them for true and honest characteristics of her personality. Some said she was a loyal friend, so I added that. The day of her funeral, the venue was filled with my Eastern Star sisters and Masonic brothers who all showed up for me because I needed support and pallbearers.

The service was eulogized by Bishop Reginald Black Sr., who is a great personal friend of mine as well as my Princelhall Mason brother. My oldest sister, Mary, and my two younger sisters, Verdell and Kaylen (Esther Jean), were in attendance. We were not able to locate the youngest of my mother's children. Kristen Latrell. To this day I don't know how long it was before she got the news of our mothers death. My mother was a member of the Junior Blind, and many of her friends from there were in attendance. I allowed everyone who wanted to give remarks to do so before me. I began my speech with, "These tears are not for Shirley Ann Tillman, these tears are for the six babies that suffered at her hands." I turned to my sisters who were seated to the left of me and said, "I'm sorry for the distance that has been created, and the wars that have been waged amongst us by our mother." I reminded them that the source of our pain is now gone, and we are now responsible for how we interact with and love each other from here on out. We can no longer blame our mother for the lives we choose to live. "She is gone," I said. "It is now up to us to build positive productive relationships with each other and live happy healthy lives and move forward."

I realize my speech in no way resembled the typical "Everyone is going to Heaven" funeral speech. I felt it was necessary for the closure I needed to continue on and finally put this all behind me. My mother's death left me with the realization that I still had a lot of healing to do.

At times, this mental and emotional transformation process is a long one. Reprogramming negative thought patterns, especially ones left by past trauma can take a long time. That is why it's best to begin working on them as soon as you identify each one. The time spent identifying and reversing negative thinking won't be in vain. It will truly change your life for the better.

One huge subconscious belief that I had to work overtime to

reverse was the fact that specific major diseases seem to run in my family. This is a common subconscious acceptance for many. Because my biological mother had diabetes, every time I experienced any bodily discomfort, I was certain it was the onset of diabetes. I no longer believe in genetic predisposition to disease.

In the book "Feeling is the Secret," by Neville Goddard, he refers to the conscious as male and the subconscious as female. He points out that the woman, being the subconscious, has no desire to change the man, being the conscious. She simply accepts him as is. The subconscious mind does not judge what we plant with our conscious actions. If you spend all of your time telling yourself that you are poor and pitiful then that is the state of mind you will remain in. The universe will create even more situations for you to feel exactly that way. You can change your state of mind.

Feeling a certain way produces that state of mind. Feeling sad will produce sadness, feeling happy will produce happiness. The minute you identify bad feelings, do everything you can to change them. Take charge of your mood.

When I read books and I find the same concepts and beliefs that I believe in today, it's always a confirmation. It makes me feel great. It confirms that I'm on the right path. It solidifies in my mind that the knowledge is real and it's not new. Many great people had this knowledge years before any of us were ever born. This knowledge is not "new aged." It's clear that many of our ancestors possessed this great information. We must always be mindful of what we are planting in our subconscious mind because our subconscious mind will produce exactly what we believe we are. If at any point we want to change the information that we are giving to the subconscious, we have to consciously take steps to create a new picture and feel the emotions related to the new positive picture we have created. Act as if the things we desire are already happening now, not in the future, but now!

It can take years to master this concept, but doing so will change your life. Hoping and wishing does not produce a happy, prosperous life. Continuously hoping and begging God for the desires of our heart is a clear representation of lack and the fact that you have accepted that limitation. Instead, mentally pretend. Believe that it is already done. Allow your prayers to be prayers of gratitude. Act as if the things you desire have already shown up in your life and soon, they will.

The mind is a magical gift from God given to us to create our lives as we choose. Embrace your Mind and its magnificent power. Whatever has shown up thus far in your life is because you have consciously or subconsciously held those thoughts in your mind. Continue to do that intentionally and you will become the master of your fate.

@In59Seconds

**The mind is like water.
When it is turbulent, it's difficult to see.
When it is calm, everything becomes clear.**

-Buddha

11

Vibrate Higher

By 2023, the phrase "vibrate high" or "raise your vibration" had become quite popular. To understand what it means to vibrate high, you first have to learn and accept that we are all vibrational beings. There is an unseen energy radiating through and around us all. When looking at or touching a human being, it does not seem that they are vibrating, but they are. All things are vibrating. Nothing is solid in the way we were once taught to believe. We are not just matter; we are energy itself, and energy is constantly evolving, responding, and interacting.

Nikola Tesla once said, "If you want to find the secrets of the universe, think in terms of energy, frequency, and vibration."

Whether people choose to accept it or dismiss it, the principle remains consistent. Everything operates on frequency. Thoughts carry frequency. Emotions carry frequency. Environments carry frequency. The conversations we entertain, the music we listen to, the people we surround ourselves with, and the beliefs we rehearse internally all contribute to the energetic signature we emit into the world. This is not mystical exaggeration. It is awareness.

Often, when we have spent a lot of time monitoring our thoughts and taking control over our lives, it causes us to become more in tune with the divine energy that surrounds and runs through us all. Whether you have gotten to the point in your life where you believe it or not, we are all energy. God is the supreme energetic source. He is not in physical form, but we are. In this human physical form, we have certain constrictions. However, as you become more in tune with the spiritual part of yourself, it becomes easier to understand that as an energetic being, even though we are confined to a physical body, we can still take control over the level of vibration we emit into the world.

That control begins in the mind.

We are all vibrating at different frequencies. The goal is to become conscious of whether you are vibrating at a higher or lower frequency at any given moment. When we are rushing, agitated, irritated, sad, fearful, or angry, we are vibrating at a lower frequency. No matter who you are—male, female, Christian, Catholic, Buddhist, adult, child, preacher, teacher, pilot, nurse—if you are walking around mad all the time, you are operating at that moment at a low vibration. Energy does not care about titles or religious affiliations. It responds to frequency.

Because of that, you will attract others that are vibrating at a similar level. If you are annoyed and complaining at work all the time, you will eventually attract another employee who feels the same way. The two of you will connect over dissatisfaction and spend your time reinforcing that shared frustration. Like attracts like. On the other hand, people who are grateful, optimistic, and solution oriented tend to gravitate toward others who reflect those same qualities. The frequency you operate on determines the company you keep.

This is where Catch and Cast becomes practical.

You cannot raise your vibration if you do not first catch the thought that lowered it.

Based on my personal experience, I have noticed that in the hustle and bustle of everyday life, we neglect to pause and truly connect with the frequencies and energies around us. Everything becomes reactionary. We respond instead of reflect. We absorb instead of assess. Once I started dedicating time to sit in stillness within a peaceful environment and focus on my breath, observation, and listening, I became aware of the frequency I was emitting in that moment. More importantly, I learned how to alter it when it was operating on a lower scale.

We focus on what is visible and neglect what is internal. If I was mad, moving too fast, or thinking negatively, I learned to stop in my tracks and turn everything off. No television. No cell phone. No radio. Silence. Then I would ask myself direct questions. What is wrong? Why are you upset? Who hurt your feelings? What expectation was not met?

That is catching the thought.

The answer did not always come instantly, but if I sat long enough, the root usually revealed itself. Sometimes it was something simple. A conversation that left me unsettled. A client who was disrespectful. One of my children acting entitled. A disappointment I had not fully processed. Identifying the precise issue helped me deal with it mentally and then choose to release it. That release is the casting.

Raising your vibration is nothing more than changing your internal dialogue before it solidifies into emotional damage.

When our lives are busy, finding stillness feels impossible. Yet even the busiest person can locate five uninterrupted minutes.

Sit in the car before turning the engine on. Stay in the bathroom stall a little longer. Close your office door. Step outside and breathe. Assess your emotional state. Check in with yourself. You are the most important person in your world, and acting as though your inner condition does not matter is a mistake. You cannot pour peace into others if chaos is dominating you internally.

I have intentionally created quiet spaces in my home and workplace. I have meditation and prayer areas where I use sound bowls, rain sticks, gongs, and guided meditation audio. The 432 Hz tone is one I return to often because it settles my nervous system and allows my thoughts to slow down. Tibetan flute music has the same effect. These tools are not magical in themselves. They simply assist in helping me regulate my internal frequency.

When the mind calms, creativity returns. Patience returns. Compassion returns. You begin operating from clarity rather than reaction. That is vibrating higher.

The daily goal is to operate from peace rather than anger, gratitude rather than fear, confidence rather than insecurity. Low frequency emotions such as resentment, hatred, jealousy, or despair will always deteriorate the quality of life if entertained long enough. We also transfer those frequencies to others without realizing it. Energy is contagious.

In this book, you are learning to identify your mood or frequency. When you recognize that you are vibrating low, it becomes your responsibility to shift it. That requires honesty.

Arguing, road rage, thoughts of self harm, hoarding out of fear, constant complaining, declaring "I'm broke," "No one loves me," or "I will probably die young" are not harmless statements. They are declarations that lower your internal frequency. Repeated often enough, they begin shaping reality.

Unfounded beliefs such as assuming you will inherit every disease in your bloodline or believing wealth is evil are mental agreements that anchor you to limitation. Millions of individuals sincerely believe they are destined for suffering. I used to think that way too.

We do not have to suffer for the sins of our parents. We do not have to inherit their fears. We do not have to accept generational limitations as permanent destiny. The power lies in the thought patterns we choose to nurture. Manifestation is not mystical wishful thinking. It is sustained focus combined with consistent action.

For many years in my twenties and thirties, I had thoughts of suicide. After losing the grandmother who raised me from three months to seventeen years old to a violent crime, I felt finished with life. Had I not learned how to elevate my vibration and Catch and Cast out those negative images of that horrible day, I would not have survived. That is not exaggeration. That is truth.

Catching the thought that says there is no hope and casting it out before it takes root can save your life.

Some reject conversations about vibration and label them as trendy language, yet energy has always existed. Across cultures around the world, the awareness of unseen forces has been acknowledged and respected. Americans are simply late to discussing it openly.

Everything is energy operating at different frequencies. I cannot claim to fully understand the mechanics of it, but I have experienced enough unexplainable events to know that unseen forces are real.

One day, I had an appointment with a spiritual therapist in

North Hollywood who specialized in Past Life Regression. I was determined to understand why I felt such an intense attachment to Phillip Clarence Morris, my youngest child's father. Despite knowing he was not healthy for me, I struggled to detach. I convinced myself that the connection must be spiritual.

When I arrived for my appointment, we spoke at length about my history with him. Just before hypnosis, I checked my phone and saw a text from him that simply said "Ready." We had not been speaking. There was no context. It was the exact word the therapist had just asked me. The timing unsettled me deeply. I could not explain it.

Whether that moment was coincidence, energy, or something beyond my understanding, it reinforced my belief that unseen connections exist.

During hypnosis, I described what appeared to be a past life. I still question whether it was memory or imagination. Regardless, it did not answer my primary question about why I felt spiritually entangled with him. What did reveal itself over time was this: I was allowing my attachment to him to lower my vibration repeatedly.

There was also a dream that shook me. After an intense disagreement, I dreamed he walked toward the door in slow motion, as if weighed down. When he touched the doorknob, a black spirit flew from his body onto mine, pinning the left side of me down. I struggled to speak until I forced out the words "The Blood of Jesus," and the weight lifted.

That dream left a lasting imprint. Whether symbolic or spiritual, it communicated something clearly. Staying energetically connected to chaos will drain you.

You do not have to fully understand the spiritual mechanics to understand the practical application. If someone repeatedly lowers your vibration, you must protect your energy. Catch the thought that romanticizes dysfunction. Cast it out. Catch the belief that you are spiritually bound to toxicity. Cast it out.

We cannot control everything that happens to us, but we can control our response. Even in chaos, you can choose to elevate your internal state. That elevation begins in the mind and expands outward.

When you are upset, pause. Breathe. Tell yourself that all things can work together for good. Meditation is a discipline that strengthens your ability to regulate your thoughts. At first your mind will wander. Stay with it. Over time, you will gain mastery over your internal dialogue.

Anger clouds judgment but calmness clarifies solutions.

The most important lesson I want you to absorb is this: your vibration is your responsibility. Eliminating people who consistently operate at low frequency is not cruelty. It is self preservation. Loving someone does not require absorbing their misery.

You are responsible for you. Pay attention to how environments make you feel. Do more of what restores you. Dance. Walk in nature. Create. Laugh. Speak kindly to yourself.

Catch the destructive thought. Cast it out before it builds momentum.

Your vibration is a choice. And choosing higher, moment by moment, is how you take your power back.

12

Forgiveness Without Self Betrayal

Some of the deepest wounds we carry are not caused by strangers. They are formed inside the relationships that were supposed to make us feel safe. Family dynamics can shape how we see ourselves in ways we do not understand until much later in life. When love is mixed with criticism, control, or unspoken expectations, the mind often absorbs those experiences as truth, even when they are not.

For a long time, I did not realize how much of my emotional suffering was tied to the need for approval. When abandonment enters a person's life early, it can create a quiet fear of being left again. That fear does not always announce itself loudly. Sometimes it shows up as people pleasing. Sometimes it shows up as perfectionism. Sometimes it shows up as an inability to say no or a constant need to prove worth.

In my own life, that dynamic played out within my family. The absence of parents created an emotional gap that I did not know how to fill. I leaned on a sibling for validation and emotional security without realizing how unhealthy that attachment had become. I placed her on a pedestal she never asked to be on, believing her approval determined my value. That belief shaped how I responded to criticism and how deeply I was hurt by it.

What I later understood is that people process pain differently. What looks like strength on the outside may simply be a different coping mechanism. My sister processed our shared experiences in a way that allowed her to appear more emotionally stable, while I internalized my pain. Neither approach was right or wrong. They were responses to the same wound.

The pain did not come from malice. It came from unexamined hurt. People often project their own unresolved pain onto those closest to them, believing they are helping, protecting, or guiding. When that projection is repeated, it can slowly erode self esteem, especially for someone already struggling with worth.

Forgiveness became necessary, not because the pain was insignificant, but because carrying it was costing me peace. Forgiveness does not mean denying the impact of what happened. It means choosing not to let it continue shaping your inner world. It means understanding intent without excusing harm. It means deciding that your healing matters more than staying stuck in resentment.

"Father forgive them for they know not what they do," Luke 23:34

Forgiveness also requires boundaries. Loving someone does not mean allowing them unlimited access to your emotional space. You can release resentment while still protecting yourself. Healthy boundaries are not punishments. They are acts of self respect.

Through the practice of Recognize, Reject, Replace, I learned to interrupt the thoughts that kept me emotionally tied to old dynamics. When critical memories surfaced, I caught them. When feelings of unworthiness appeared, I rejected the lie. When the urge to seek validation returned, I replaced it with truth. I reminded myself that my value was not dependent on anyone else's approval.

Reclaiming emotional freedom means taking responsibility for how you allow others to live inside your mind. You cannot control what people say or do, but you can control how long their words echo internally. That is where freedom lives.

Family relationships are complex. Love and pain often coexist. Healing does not require cutting everyone out of your life. It requires clarity, compassion, and self authority. When you learn to respond from awareness instead of old wounds, you begin to relate differently. You stop shrinking. You stop over explaining. You stop abandoning yourself to keep the peace.

Forgiveness is not a single moment. It is a practice. Each time an old thought returns, you have an opportunity to choose differently. That choice weakens the pattern and strengthens your sense of self.

In the next chapter, we will focus on taking your power back fully and learning how to live from intention instead of reaction.

13

Taking Your Power Back

I used to be poor but not financially, I was poor my spirit and my faith. Most importantly I had a poverty mindset, which is something that many people struggle with.

I was emotionally depleted because of the things I had been through in my past. I now know that God did not intend for us to suffer or struggle mentally, spiritually, emotionally or financially. But then I had no idea of that fact. We were created from love and this universe we live in is abundant and it is ready and waiting to bestow that abundance upon us.We are supposed to experience wealth in all areas of our lives. Mental, physical, financial and emotional abundance can all be ours once we learn to break free from all of our limiting beliefs. Financial abundance is something many of us want, but most of us don't believe we can actually have it. We must become rich mentally and emotionally before we can attain financial abundance. Otherwise we won't be able to sustain it because we won't believe we deserve it. Once we fall in love with ourselves and stop tormenting ourselves with past events, and accept that we deserve the best that life has to offer our finances will follow suit. Therefore becoming spiritually rich must take precedence.

Most of our parents and grandparents had a poverty mindset. They believed we were destined to develop the diseases of our ancestors. Many of them who were very religious didn't believe in wealth or financial abundance they believed it to be a sin of greed. They believed that you worked really hard to make just enough money just to get by.

They were great people, It's not their fault they sincerely didn't know any better. Ideas of abundant wealth had not been taught to them. They could not even imagine it nor were they aware that the absence of wealth had anything to do with them and the limitations they unconsciously excepted for their lives.

It's just an example of how our minds can be conditioned to accept lack and limitations. Those mental limitations were implanted into the minds of each generation that followed. Now that we know better we can change those thoughts patterns. Now that we are aware of the great power we have to create through our thoughts we can now learn and teach our children and our children's children to adopt a way of thinking that embraces and welcomes prosperity, happiness,love, great health and abundant wealth into our lives. We can have all of it. We do not have to sacrifice one for the other. We do not have to abandon the idea of being rich in all areas of our live to be closer to God. The amazing divine source that created us is for us not against us.

Allowing myself to learn a more positive way of thinking changed my life tremendously. This new way of thinking allowed me to access my God-given power, one that we all possess. This power comes from within us and it is limitless, timeless and abundant.

I want everyone who reads this book to learn effective tools to tap into their own power. Once one acquires the knowledge and begins to utilize this internal power they become fearless and invincible. They come to realize that all things are possible and there is absolutely nothing that you can not do. Once you transform your mindset from poverty to power you will begin to see progress in all areas of your life.

The only limitations that truly exist are the ones we choose to accept in our minds.

We live in different times now. We have more resources and access to greater knowledge than our ancestors did. I believe it was the prayer of our ancestors that we eventually learn this valuable information to assist in the overall advancement of mankind.

It's vital that we gain and apply the insight so that we can motivate the generations that follow us. The children are indeed our future. I feel it is our job to teach them that they are creators. We must inspire them to strive harder, set larger goals and to not stop until they have achieved them. We must set the example and pave the way by first utilizing our tools to advance our own lives to the fullest. We can start by tapping into our own power and changing our poverty mindset and teaching our children and our children's children that they can do anything. Mental poverty can lead to poverty in all other areas of our lives. We can not sustainably transform one without the other. The mindset shift come first. Once we reset our mind and learn to positively guide our thoughts our lives will change for the better.

We have all heard the popular phrase or song "Free your mind and the rest will follow" Well I like to switch the words up a bit and say "Free Your Mind and You Will Follow". The true you that was intended to live a wonderful happy boundless life. Once we learn to free our mind from all the negative lies that prevent us from prospering we will then experience our true inherent greatness.

I am the mother of four children, three girls and one boy. They have been the driving force behind my desire to live a more fulfilling life. I wanted to be certain my children never felt abandoned, hurt or unwanted. I worked hard as a small business owner for over 23 years to ensure they were taken care of financially. That part was easy for me. The challenge for me was to finally step back and look at my life and realize there was still so much mental and emotional work that needed to be done.

I loved my babies so much, but deep inside I was afraid. I was so afraid that they would get hurt and it was hard for me to allow them to participate in normal childhood things. I needed them and i was afraid of losing them. I was loving them through my fear. I wanted them with me at all times so I could protect them, but anyone who has children knows that once they get older they rebel from that constant smothering.

A friend of mind once explained to me that our children are gifts from God, but they aren't ours. We were simply blessed enough to be the portal that the divine source allowed them to come through. They are here on earth to have their own life experiences. This revelation helped me to back up a little and allow them to live their own lives without my dictation. Anytime I felt the urge to smother them, I would remind myself that they belong to God and no matter what they are going to experience life on their own terms. I realized that there was not much I personally could do to prevent them from being hurt mentally or physically because human beings were placed here to create their own lives. As parents, it may be difficult sometimes, but we have to sit back and allow them to live. Being a mother who had so many wounds of her own, giving them the space they needed to grow and learn was sometimes easier said than done.

I love being a mother, and if I could do it over again I would have 10 children.

I am elated that I did the emotional work needed so that I can have the productive relationships I desired with my children. I am so happy that I now possess the knowledge that we create our own destiny. Our thoughts play the largest part in that. Our imagination is a gift given to us from God to create the best life experience possible. I teach my children that they have no limits other than the ones they set for themselves. A quote of my own that I have drilled into my 6-year-old is:

Y*our life is like a coloring book and only you have the crayons.*

Being a parent is something I have always been grateful for, although my children were like bandaids in the beginning,. They literally masked my holes and emotional wounds and made me temporarily forget the pain of my past. When each one would get older and not need me as much, that band aid would slowly begin to peel off and I would find myself in pain again, feeling unloved and unworthy, so I would have another baby. I wanted to create little people of my own that I was certain would love me unconditionally, such a burden for them to be responsible for my happiness, even though most of their lives they had no idea of the painful baggage I had been carrying.

It wasn't until I became a motivational speaker that my children ever heard my entire story. I felt it was to dark and depressing to share with happy hopeful innocent children. Every now and then one of them would ask me " Mommy, where is your mommy?" I found clever ways to give them satisfactory answers until I was ready to explain my past to them. It wasn't that I thought they would feel differently about me, I simply didn't want them to know such horrible things happen in the world.

There is something sacred about childhood. It carries a softness that the world is too quick to harden. When my children would ask about my mother, the question was simple to them, but heavy for me. They were not asking out of suspicion or confusion. They were asking out of curiosity. Out of love. Out of a natural desire to understand their family tree. Yet behind that innocent question lived memories I had spent years trying to bury.

I was not ashamed of my story. I was protective of their innocence.

As a mother, you want your children to believe that the world is safe. You want them to believe that bad things are rare and that love is the default setting of humanity. I had lived long enough to know that love is powerful, but so is pain. I did not want to introduce them to darkness before their time.

Eventually I set out on a desperate mission to seek healing. Being raised in the church by my grandmother, that had been the first stop in my desperate dash to finally rid myself of my pain. I did what many call church hopping.

When the pain becomes louder than your pride, you start searching. You start looking for relief anywhere it might exist. For me, church was familiar ground. It was where I learned about faith. It was where I learned about hope. It was where I first heard that victory was possible even when circumstances looked impossible.

I was raised in a church in Compton, California, called Ephesians Church of God In Christ, or "C.O.G.I.C." My grandmother was very active in the church. She was part of the mothers' board and every Sunday she stood in front of the congregation and sang a song. I can still close my eyes and remember her singing,

"The fight is on, The trumpet sound is ringing out, The cry to arms, Is heard far and near the Lord of host, Is Marching on to victory."

When I think of my grandmother, I think of strength wrapped in gentleness and just pure love. I think of kind discipline and prayer. A woman who carried her own pain but refused to let it define her posture. That song was not just lyrics. It was a declaration and a reminder that life is a fight, but the fight is not without purpose.

As a little girl sitting in those pews, I did not fully understand what it meant to fight spiritually. I only knew that my grandmother believed in victory. Her voice would fill the sanctuary, steady and unwavering. Even now, when I close my eyes, I can hear her. I can see her standing tall, singing as though she already knew the outcome.

Years later, when I found myself in the deepest, darkest place emotionally, the only tool I possessed at the time was the ability to go to church. So back to the church I ran desperately.

Desperation strips away pride. It does not care about appearances. It does not care about what people think. It only cares about survival. I was not looking for religion. I was looking for relief. I was not looking for performance. I was looking for peace.

So I sat in different pews. I listened to different sermons. I lifted my hands in different sanctuaries. I prayed prayers that were not polished. I cried tears that had been stored up for years. I believed that if I could just find the right building, the right preacher, the right choir, something inside of me would shift. Church hopping was not rebellion on my part. It was searching for healing.

But here is what I eventually learned. Healing does not come from geography. It does not come from a new address or a new congregation or church home. It does not come from louder music or longer sermons. It comes from within.

Later I would come to realize that the healing I needed starts within. Until a person is done reliving the past and finally accepts that its their choice not to, it's not much any person or organization can do to help them. Suffering begins in the mind and it is a choice we do not have to make. Acknowledging that was the beginning of my new life. That realization was both empowering and terrifying.

Empowering because it meant I was not powerless. Terrifying because it meant I could no longer blame anyone else for my healing. The truth is, pain can become comfortable. It becomes familiar. You learn how to function with it. You learn how to decorate it. You learn how to speak from it. But as long as you are reliving it, you are giving it authority over your present. Taking your power back begins with a decision.

It begins when you recognize that you cannot change what happened, but you can change what you rehearse. Every time we replay a traumatic memory, we relive it. The body responds as though it is happening again. The heart tightens. The stomach turns. The mind spirals. Catching that thought and casting it out is not denial. It is discipline.

For years, I rehearsed my pain. I told myself the story of what happened to me over and over again. I wore it like a garment.

I allowed it to inform how I trusted, how I loved, how I saw myself. I did not realize that I was strengthening the very chains I wanted broken. Taking your power back means interrupting that cycle.

It means saying, yes, this happened, but it does not own me. It means acknowledging the wound without worshiping it. It means understanding that your mind is powerful enough to create suffering even after the event has passed. Suffering begins in the mind. That sentence changed my life.

Circumstances may introduce pain, but suffering is prolonged when we continue to engage with thoughts that weaken us. That does not mean we pretend nothing happened. It means we choose not to live there anymore.

The church gave me language. It gave me faith. It reminded me that victory was possible. But it was in the quiet moments, alone with my thoughts, that the real work began. I had to confront the narrative I had built around my pain. I had to challenge the lies I believed about myself. I had to ask myself whether I was ready to let go of the identity of victim and step into the identity of survivor. That is where power lives.

Power is not loud. It does not always look dramatic. Sometimes it looks like a woman sitting alone, deciding that she will no longer allow yesterday to dictate tomorrow. Sometimes it looks like choosing not to answer a thought that tries to drag you backward. Sometimes it looks like forgiveness, not because the offender deserves it, but because you deserve freedom.

When I finally accepted that healing was my responsibility, everything changed. I stopped running from church to church looking for someone to fix me. I started doing the inner work. I started catching the negative thoughts when they surfaced. I started casting out the lies that told me I was broken beyond repair. That was the beginning of my new life.

Not the day I became a motivational speaker. Not the day I told my children my full story. Not the day I stood on a stage. It began the moment I realized that my mind was not my enemy unless I allowed it to be.

Taking your power back is not about denying the past. It is about refusing to give it your future. Once I understood that, I was no longer desperate.

I was determined.

14

Practice, Not Perfection

Real change does not happen in a single moment of clarity. It happens through repetition, patience, and commitment. One of the biggest mistakes people make when trying to heal their thinking patterns is believing they need to get it right all the time. That belief alone can become another source of pressure and self judgment. This work is not about perfection. It is about practice.

When you begin applying Recognize, Reject, Replace consistently, you will notice progress, not instant transformation. Some days you will catch a thought the moment it enters your mind. Other days you will realize it hours later. Both moments matter. Both count. Every time you notice a thought and choose to respond differently, you are weakening an old pattern and strengthening a new one.

At first, replacing a negative thought with a positive one can feel uncomfortable or even false. When you have spent years believing something about yourself, introducing a new belief can feel unnatural. That does not mean the new thought is wrong. It means it is unfamiliar. Familiarity has nothing to do with truth. It only reflects repetition.

Practice teaches the mind what you want it to learn. Each time you interrupt a harmful thought, you send a message to yourself that your inner world matters. Each time you choose a supportive thought, you reinforce safety, worth, and self respect. Over time, those choices begin to feel more natural. The mind adapts to what it is consistently shown.

There will be moments when old thoughts return with intensity. This does not mean you have failed or regressed. It means you are human. Stress, fatigue, and emotional triggers can reactivate patterns temporarily. What matters is how you respond when that happens. Do not punish yourself. Return to awareness. Catch the thought. Cast it out. Replace it with intention.

Consistency is more powerful than effort. Small daily practices create lasting change. This may look like pausing throughout the day to check in with your thoughts. It may look like repeating affirmations that feel supportive. It may look like sitting in silence and allowing yourself to observe without judgment. The form does not matter as much as the commitment.

This work extends beyond individual thoughts. It changes how you relate to yourself. You become more compassionate. More patient. More grounded. You stop expecting yourself to be healed overnight and start honoring the process. That shift alone can bring relief.

Practice also builds trust. You begin to trust yourself to handle what arises. You stop fearing your own mind because you know you have tools. You know that even when difficult thoughts appear, they do not get the final word.

Learning to Catch and Cast and implementing the Recognize,

Reject, Replace system is not something you complete. It is something you live daily. It becomes a way of engaging with your inner world that supports growth instead of fear. Over time, it changes not only how you think, but how you feel, respond, and how you move through life.

15

Conclusion

Your Mind Is Your Home - You Hold the Power

If there is one thing I hope remains with you long after you close this book, it is this: you are not powerless in your own mind. No matter what you have been through, no matter how long you have struggled, no matter how convincing your fears, doubts, and painful memories may seem, there has always been a part of you that is greater than the thoughts that pass through your awareness. That power was never taken from you. It was never destroyed. It was never absent. It may have been buried beneath years of conditioning, trauma, fear, disappointment, and self doubt, but it remained there waiting for you to recognize it.

For much of my life, I did not understand this. I believed my thoughts were simply happening to me. When fear appeared, I felt afraid. When shame surfaced, I accepted it as truth. When painful memories replayed themselves in my mind, I assumed I had no choice but to relive them over and over again. I did not realize that my attention was feeding the very things that were causing me suffering. I did not understand that every thought I entertained, rehearsed, and emotionally invested in was strengthening a pathway that would become easier to travel again tomorrow. Like many people, I confused familiarity with truth. I thought because a thought appeared often, it must be accurate. I thought because an emotion felt strong, it must be permanent.

What this journey taught me is that thoughts only gain power when they are believed, repeated, and protected. Left unquestioned, they become stories. Those stories become identities. Those identities become prisons. Before long, a person can spend years living inside a narrative that was never true to begin with. The mind has an incredible ability to create suffering when it is left unattended. Yet the same mind possesses an equally incredible ability to create healing when it is guided with awareness, compassion, and intention.

Some of you reading this have survived experiences that changed you. Some have carried burdens that no one else fully understands. There may be wounds that still ache when you think about them. There may be memories that still make your chest tighten. There may be moments from your past that continue to visit you when you least expect them. I want you to hear this clearly. What happened to you matters. Your pain mattered. Your grief mattered. Your fear mattered. The experiences that shaped you were real, and acknowledging that reality is an important part of healing.

Yet what happened to you is not who you are.

The worst moments of your life are chapters in your story, but they are not the author of it. Trauma is something that happened. Loss is something that happened. Betrayal is something that happened. Fear is something that happened. None of those things have the authority to define your future unless you continue handing them that authority in the present. There is a profound difference between carrying a memory and allowing that memory to carry you. One honors the past. The other remains trapped inside it.

This is why the practice of Catch and Cast matters so deeply. It is not simply a technique. It is a way of reclaiming ownership of your inner world. Every time you catch a thought, you interrupt an unconscious pattern. Every time you cast out a belief that no longer serves you, you weaken its hold over your life. Every time you replace fear with truth, self criticism with compassion, or hopelessness with possibility, you are teaching your mind a new way to exist. These moments may seem small while they are happening, but lives are changed through small moments repeated consistently over time.

You do not need perfection for this process to work. You do not need to reach a point where negative thoughts never appear. You do not need to become someone who is unaffected by challenges, disappointment, or uncertainty. You are human. Thoughts will continue to arise. Emotions will continue to move through you. Difficult seasons will still come and go. The goal was never to eliminate every uncomfortable thought from your mind. The goal is to stop giving those thoughts complete authority over your life.

There will be days when awareness comes easily and days when it feels like a struggle. Some mornings you will notice a negative thought immediately and replace it with something healthier. Other days you may catch yourself halfway through an old pattern and realize you have been mentally rehearsing fear for hours. Neither experience means you are succeeding or failing. Both are part of the process. Growth rarely arrives in a straight line. Healing unfolds layer by layer, revealing deeper levels of freedom each time you choose awareness over autopilot.

Whenever you stumble, remember this. The fact that you noticed means you are already making progress. Awareness itself is evidence of growth. Years ago, you may have lived inside certain thought patterns without ever questioning them. Today, you are learning to recognize them. Tomorrow, you will become even quicker at catching them. Change is often invisible while it is happening. Then one day you find yourself responding differently to situations that once controlled you, and you realize you are no longer the same person who started this journey.

I also want you to remember that your worth has never been determined by the quality of your thoughts. You are not more valuable on the days when you feel confident, and you are not less valuable on the days when you struggle. Your value does not rise and fall with your emotions. It does not depend on your productivity, your achievements, your appearance, your past mistakes, or anyone else's opinion of you. You were created with purpose. You were created with dignity. You were created with value that existed long before fear ever entered the picture.

God did not create you to spend your life imprisoned by shame, anxiety, self hatred, or hopelessness. He created you with the capacity to think, choose, learn, grow, and heal. He gave you the ability to observe your mind rather than become enslaved by it. He gave you awareness so that you could recognize what is true and release what is not. The power you have been searching for has never been somewhere outside of you. It has been quietly waiting within you all along.

As you move forward from this book, I hope you give yourself the same compassion you would offer someone you deeply love.

Real healing is rarely dramatic. Most of the time it unfolds quietly through small decisions that seem insignificant while they are happening. A single moment of awareness. A choice not to believe a thought that once controlled you. A willingness to pause before reacting. An act of kindness toward yourself on a day when self criticism would have been easier. These moments rarely feel life changing when they occur, yet they are the very moments that shape a new future. Lasting transformation is not built through grand breakthroughs. It is built through consistent choices that gradually teach the mind a different way to exist.

The journey ahead will not be perfect, nor does it need to be. Some days you will feel strong, clear, and deeply connected to the truth of who you are. Other days old fears may return unexpectedly and familiar patterns may attempt to reclaim their place in your mind. Neither experience defines your progress. Growth is not measured by the absence of struggle. It is measured by your ability to meet those struggles differently than you once did. What matters is not whether difficult thoughts appear. What matters is whether you continue to hand them authority over your life. Awareness gives you the ability to recognize them. Wisdom gives you the ability to question them. Practice gives you the ability to choose something better.

Throughout these pages, I have shared a simple idea that has the power to change everything when applied consistently. The thoughts that create suffering do not deserve unrestricted access to your mind simply because they appear there. You have the ability to notice them. You have the ability to challenge them. You have the ability to decide which thoughts deserve your attention and which ones deserve to be released. Every time you refuse to participate in a cycle of fear, shame, resentment, self hatred, or hopelessness, you strengthen a different pathway. Every time you choose truth over distortion, compassion over criticism, or hope over despair, you are reclaiming territory that once felt lost.

Perhaps the most important thing I have learned is that the mind becomes whatever it repeatedly practices. When fear is rehearsed every day, fear grows stronger. When peace is practiced every day, peace grows stronger. The same principle applies to self worth, confidence, gratitude, forgiveness, and love. Whatever receives your attention receives your energy. Whatever receives your energy begins to shape your experience of life. This is why the practice of Catch and Cast matters so deeply. It is not about controlling every thought that enters your awareness. It is about becoming intentional about which thoughts are allowed to stay.

Your mind is the environment in which every experience of your life takes place. Long after the circumstances around you change, long after certain people leave and new seasons arrive, your relationship with yourself remains. That relationship deserves care. It deserves patience. It deserves honesty. Most importantly, it deserves protection. The home you carry within you should not be a place where fear is allowed to dominate every room. It should be a place where truth is welcomed, where grace is available, where hope is nurtured, and where healing has the space to grow.

As I bring this book to a close, I want to leave you with the same truth that changed my own life. You are not trapped by your past. You are not defined by your wounds. You are not condemned to repeat every thought that has ever crossed your mind. Beneath the noise, beneath the fear, beneath the stories that suffering sometimes convinces us to believe, there is still a part of you that remains whole. There is still a part of you capable of choosing differently. There is still a part of you connected to peace, wisdom, and the presence of God.

That part of you has been there all along. Trust it and listen to it. Allow it to guide you forward.

The next chapter of your life is not determined by what happened yesterday. It is shaped by what you choose to believe, practice, and nurture today. Every thought you catch creates an opportunity. Every thought you cast away creates space. Every moment of awareness opens a new possibility. Over time those moments become habits, those habits become character, and that character becomes the foundation of a life lived with greater peace, freedom, and purpose.

Your story is still being written. The pages ahead have not been decided yet. What happens next is completely up to you.

About the Author

SaBrina Fisher Reece understands what it means to keep going without applause.

For more than twenty six years, she built one of the most influential braiding salons and schools in Los Angeles, Braids By SaBrina, earning recognition throughout California as The Braid Queen. Her name was on the door, her reputation was on the line, and her success was self built. Behind the achievements, however, was a quieter truth. Much of her journey was navigated without consistent support, validation, or encouragement from others.

SaBrina's life has been shaped by early abandonment, profound loss, and the slow, intentional development of self trust. Those experiences taught her that confidence on the outside does not always mean peace on the inside, and that real strength is often learned when you are forced to become your own support system.

Today, SaBrina is an author, speaker, and guide devoted to emotional growth, self mastery, and inner alignment. She is the author of multiple transformational works, including *My Spiritual Smile: Tools for Mental and Emotional Transformation, Your Mind Is Magic, Perfectly Positive: How to Stay Positive When Life Is Not Perfect, Spiritual Balance: Aligning Mind, Body, and Energy in Everyday Life, Living Life on a Higher Frequency, How to Get Exactly What You Want From God, Kicking Depression in the Butt, Self Sabotage, Become Your Own Cheerleader, Family Fun Night Cookbook, When I Say I Am, How to Make More Money in 2026,* and *Over Fifty and Still Fine, Looking to Date Again.* Each book reflects a chapter of her own evolution and healing.

Now residing in New Mexico, SaBrina continues her work through writing, sound healing practices, and helping others bring their literary dreams to life through In59Seconds Publishing Co. She consistently reminds readers that there is no single path to peace, only the courage to walk your own.

Her message is simple and unwavering.

Sometimes the most important applause you will ever receive is the one you give yourself.

You can connect with me on:
🌐 https://in59secondspublishing.com

Also by Bri Reece

SaBrina Fisher Reece writes self-help books rooted in emotional healing, personal growth, and spiritual awareness. Her work blends lived experience with motivational insight, often exploring themes of balance, resilience, self-mastery, and the unseen forces that shape our thoughts and behaviors. Drawing from both practical reflection and metaphysical concepts, her writing encourages readers to develop greater self-awareness, reconnect with their inner strength, and create more intentional, aligned live

Kicking Depression in the Butt

Kicking Depression in the Butt is a raw, faith-infused, and deeply practical guide for anyone who is tired of surviving in silence and ready to reclaim their life.

Drawing from her own lived experiences with trauma, abandonment, loss, and depression, SaBrina Fisher Reece invites readers into an honest conversation about what depression really feels like,and how to fight back. This book does not minimize pain or offer shallow positivity. Instead, it helps readers recognize depression as an internal enemy, interrupt destructive thought cycles, and rebuild their inner world with intention, truth, and daily tools that actually work.

Through personal storytelling, spiritual insight, and mindset-shifting strategies, SaBrina shows readers how to stop identifying with their darkest thoughts and begin designing a life that protects their peace. She addresses the realities of trauma, triggers, boundaries, faith, therapy, medication, and personal responsibility, offering a balanced approach that honors both professional support and inner work.

Kicking Depression in the Butt is for the person who keeps showing up while quietly falling apart. It is for those who smile while suffering, who feel strong on the outside but exhausted on the inside. Most of all, it is a reminder that depression may visit, but it does not get to stay, and it does not get to become your identity.

This book is not about perfection. It's about progress. It's about learning how to fight for your mind, your peace, and your future, one thought, one choice, and one day at a time.

Because as long as you have breath in your body, your story is not over, and you still have the power to kick depression in the butt.

Over 50 and Still Fine
Over 50 and Still Fine: Looking to Date Again explores the realities of midlife dating with honesty, humor, and emotional depth. In this reflective and empowering work, author SaBrina Fisher Reece examines the healing process required to re-enter the dating world after loss, long-term relationships, or extended periods of self-focus.

Blending personal experiences with insight and encouragement, the book addresses the emotional challenges, shifting expectations, and renewed self-awareness that often accompany dating later in life. Rather than offering a formula for romance, Reece emphasizes self-worth, emotional clarity, and the importance of honoring one's boundaries while remaining open to connection.

This book speaks to readers seeking authenticity, growth, and laughter as they navigate the evolving landscape of relationships. **Over 50 and Still Fine** affirms that dating at any age can be a meaningful extension of self-discovery, healing, and personal empowerment.

The Balance & Focus Series

The Balance & Focus Series is designed to help readers return to themselves in a world that constantly pulls them off center. These books explore two essential elements of a grounded, intentional life: inner balance and conscious focus.

Balance examines how alignment between mind, body, and energy creates stability, emotional clarity, and resilience, even during life's most challenging moments. *Focus* builds on that foundation by exploring the power of attention, intention, and mental discipline, showing how clarity and direction shape the outcomes we experience.

Together, these books offer practical insight and spiritual awareness for those seeking to live with greater purpose, presence, and self-mastery. This series is not about perfection, but about learning how to steady yourself, direct your energy wisely, and create a life that feels aligned from the inside out.

The World Is Ready
The World Is Ready: A Gentle Awakening to Sound, Energy, and the Spiritual Self is a compassionate invitation for those who sense there is more to life than what they were taught to see, yet still wish to honor their faith, their upbringing, and their reverence for God.

Written for readers raised within structured religious traditions, this book offers a safe and respectful bridge into spiritual practices that support balance, healing, and inner awareness. It reassures the reader that exploring sound healing, breathwork, meditation, grounding, and energy awareness is not a betrayal of faith, but a natural expansion of it.

Through deeply personal experiences, including recovery from major surgery supported by sound, private sound healing sessions, and sacred encounters in spiritual sites across the world, the author gently illustrates how ancient practices and modern understanding meet. From binaural beats and tuning forks to healing crystals, chakras, breath as life force, and the quiet power of the mind, each chapter unfolds with warmth, clarity, and emotional honesty.

This book does not preach, persuade, or pressure. Instead, it speaks softly to the soul, honoring curiosity while dissolving fear. It recognizes that spirituality does not belong to one religion, culture, or language, but lives within the shared human experience of seeking peace, connection, and meaning.

The World Is Ready is for anyone who has ever felt drawn to spiritual exploration but hesitated out of loyalty, doubt, or uncertainty. It affirms that spiritual practices are not witchcraft or rebellion, but tools of awareness that help us return to balance, regulate the nervous system, and remember our true nature.

This is not a call to abandon belief.

It is an invitation to remember who you are.

The world is ready.

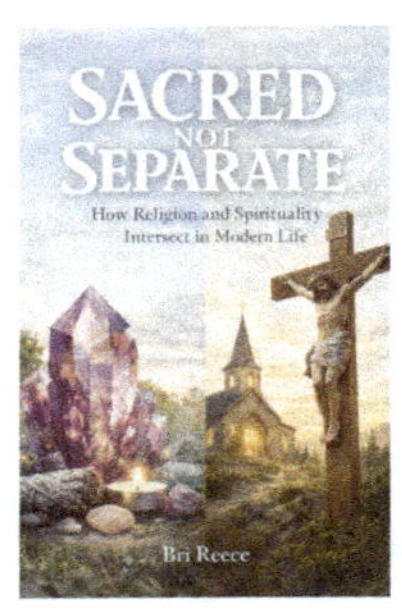

Sacred, Not Separate
How Religion and Spirituality Interact in Modern Life:

What if the line between religion and spirituality was never meant to divide us?

In a world where people argue over doctrine, label one another, and separate themselves based on belief systems, *Sacred, Not Separate* offers a deeply personal and unifying perspective. This book is not about choosing sides. It is about bridging them.

Raised in the Christian Church of God in Christ by her grandmother, Bri Reece grew up rooted in faith, gospel music, prayer, and reverence for God. Later, through world travel, personal trauma, spiritual exploration, and profound healing experiences, she encountered meditation, sound healing, breath work, and ancient earth based practices that expanded her understanding of the divine.

Instead of abandoning religion for spirituality, or rejecting spirituality for religion, she discovered something powerful:

They are not enemies.

They are expressions.

Through raw storytelling and emotional honesty, Bri explores:

The illusion of division between church and spiritual practice

The power of sound in both gospel worship and sound healing

How trauma can make us vulnerable to spiritual ego

The importance of discernment in both religious institutions and spiritual centers

Breath as the universal bridge between body and spirit

Why meditation and prayer are more alike than we think

How belief shapes our lived experience

Why love is the only true spiritual barometer

This book courageously addresses spiritual manipulation, grief, healing, world travel, cultural perspective, and the personal responsibility we all carry in creating peace. It challenges the idea that God belongs to one structure, one language, or one group of people.

If your beliefs make you kinder, they are aligned.

If they make you cruel, something is off.

It is that simple.

Sacred, Not Separate is for the person who loves Jesus but also meditates.

For the one who wears a cross and a crystal.

For the family member tired of arguing at the dinner table.

For the seeker who refuses to be boxed in.

This is not a debate.

It is a bridge.

If you are ready to embrace unity without losing your foundation, to deepen your faith without shrinking your curiosity, and to live from a place of one God and one love, this book will meet you exactly where you are.

The sacred was never separate.

We just forgot.

Is This Why They Burned The Books? (EBook)
Buried Wisdom from the Past

What if the most powerful knowledge was never destroyed... only buried?

Across history, libraries have burned, philosophers have been silenced, and ancient civilizations have disappeared. Yet fragments of their wisdom continue to surface in unexpected places. In sacred geometry carved into stone. In healing traditions rooted in the earth. In philosophies that challenge us to master the mind. In spiritual teachings that insist the kingdom is within.

In *Is This Why They Burned the Books?*, Bri Reece takes readers on a deeply personal and thought provoking journey through ancient Egypt, Peru, and Greece, exploring the possibility that humanity once understood more about consciousness, energy, and inner power than we acknowledge today.

Drawing from travel experiences inside the Great Pyramid of Giza, meditation above Machu Picchu, and reflections in Delphi and Meteora, this book bridges ancient civilizations with modern self awareness. It asks bold but balanced questions:

What did our ancestors know about the mind?

Why do certain ideas about human potential keep resurfacing across centuries?

Are we operating at only a fraction of our true capacity?

What does evolving to a higher self actually look like?

This is not a conspiracy book. It is a curiosity book.

It does not attack religion. It expands perspective.

It does not claim certainty. It invites exploration.

Through thoughtful reflection on ancient wisdom, energy,

grounding, inner discipline, and the vastness of the universe, Bri Reece offers readers something far more valuable than answers. She offers responsibility. The responsibility to think deeply, to seek humbly, and to remember that human potential is far from exhausted.

If you have ever felt that there is more to this life than routine and repetition...

If you are a seeker who questions without arrogance...

If you sense that buried wisdom is waiting to be rediscovered...

This book is for you. The fire may have burned the pages. But the wisdom remains.

How Do I Control My emotions

When Anger, Rage, and Impulsive Behavior Is Destroying Your Life:

Anger does not make you powerful. It makes you reactive. And unchecked reactions can quietly dismantle your relationships, your health, your career, and your peace.

In **How Do I Control My Emotions?**, author and transformational voice **SaBrina Fisher Reece** takes you on a deeply honest journey through emotional self-mastery. Drawing from her own lived experiences as a business owner, leader, and woman who once wore anger as armor, SaBrina exposes the real roots of rage, impulsive behavior, and emotional outbursts—and shows you how to take your power back.

This book is not about suppressing emotions or pretending everything is fine. It is about understanding why you react the way you do, identifying hidden triggers tied to abandonment, trauma, and unmet needs, and learning how to pause, choose, and respond with intention instead of regret.

Inside these pages, you will learn:

Why anger feels justified in the moment but costs you in the long run

How unhealed pain disguises itself as control, dominance, or intensity

The difference between reacting and responding

Why emotional discipline is a form of self-respect

How to stop letting your past control your present

Written with compassion, clarity, and accountability, this book is a call to action for anyone tired of apologizing, repairing damage, or living with the consequences of emotional explosions. If you are ready to stop being ruled by anger and start living from self-control, awareness, and peace, this book will meet you exactly where you are.

You cannot control other people.

But you can always control **you**.

And that changes everything.

Second by Second (EBook)

Daily Tools to Co-Create a Great Life explores the concept that human beings actively shape their reality through thought, emotion, and intentional focus.

Drawing from spiritual principles, practical psychology, and personal experience, Bri Reece presents a structured approach to conscious co-creation. The book emphasizes the power of visualization, emotional alignment, and disciplined thought management as daily tools for personal transformation.

Through relatable stories and accessible instruction, readers learn how to:

Recognize and redirect limiting thought patterns

Use imagination as a creative instrument

Align emotion with desired outcomes

Integrate spiritual belief with personal responsibility

Reece presents co-creation as a partnership between the individual and the divine, offering readers a framework for intentional living grounded in faith, awareness, and consistent practice.

This book is designed for readers interested in personal development, spirituality, mindset mastery, and practical tools for self-directed growth.

Remaining Human

Protecting Your Authenticity in the Era of Artificial Intelligence

We are living in the most technologically advanced era in human history, yet so many people have never felt more emotionally disconnected, spiritually exhausted, or alone.

In *Remaining Human*, author SaBrina Fisher Reece delivers a deeply emotional and thought provoking exploration of what it means to protect the heart, soul, and authentic human experience in a world increasingly consumed by artificial intelligence, social media, constant stimulation, and digital distraction. This is not a book written against technology. It is a powerful reminder that advancement should never come at the cost of human connection, emotional intimacy, spiritual grounding, or the God given parts of ourselves that make life meaningful.

Through raw reflection, heartfelt storytelling, spiritual insight, and conversations about everything from AI to family connection, Nikola Tesla, emotional exhaustion, social media, children growing up in a digital world, and the sacred importance of human touch, this book invites readers back to what truly matters.

Inside these pages, readers will rediscover:

The importance of emotional presence in a distracted world

Why human touch, love, and connection still matter deeply

How technology is reshaping relationships, families, and identity

The emotional consequences of over-stimulation and artificial living

The spiritual importance of remaining grounded in God

How to embrace innovation without losing your humanity

Why authenticity, compassion, creativity, and emotional depth are worth protecting

Written with warmth, honesty, wisdom, and compassion, *Remaining Human* speaks directly to the soul of anyone who feels overwhelmed by the pace of modern life and longs to reconnect with peace, purpose, family, love, and genuine human connection again.

This book is not about fearing the future.

It is about refusing to lose yourself inside of it.

Start Your Day with Grounding (EBOOK ONLY)

A Gentle Guide to Reconnecting with Earth, Peace, and Presence

is a heartfelt invitation to slow down, reconnect with nature, and rediscover the peace that has been waiting beneath your feet all along.

In a world filled with noise, stress, endless scrolling, and emotional exhaustion, this book gently reminds readers that some of the most powerful forms of healing, clarity, and inner peace are still beautifully simple. Through grounding, the practice of placing your bare feet on the Earth, author Sabrina Fisher Reece shares a deeply personal and spiritual journey of reconnecting with nature, presence, gratitude, and God's creation.

Inspired by transformative experiences in Bali, Peru, Egypt, and beyond, this book explores the emotional, spiritual, and wellness benefits of grounding while encouraging readers to create small daily rituals that bring more calm, balance, and connection into their lives. From peaceful mornings in the grass to barefoot walks along the beach, grounding becomes more than a wellness practice. It becomes a return to stillness, simplicity, and self.

Inside this book, readers will discover:

The emotional and spiritual benefits of grounding

How nature helps calm the nervous system and restore balance

Scientific research and wellness perspectives surrounding

grounding practices

Personal travel stories and reflections from sacred places around the world

The connection between grounding, gratitude, and presence

Ways families, children, couples, and individuals can incorporate grounding into everyday life

Gentle encouragement for creating peaceful rituals in a fast paced world

Written with warmth, compassion, and spiritual depth, Start Your Day with Grounding does not promise perfection or miracle cures. Instead, it offers readers something far more meaningful: a simple, free, natural practice that may help them feel calmer, clearer, more connected, and more alive.

If you have ever felt peaceful walking barefoot on the beach, calmer after time spent in nature, or emotionally restored beneath the warmth of the sun, then you have already experienced the quiet power of grounding.

Now it is time to bring that feeling into your everyday life.

How to Balance Good and Evil Understanding the Polarity of Human Nature and Choosing the Higher Path

What if "good" and "evil" are not distant forces fighting somewhere outside of you-but daily choices happening quietly within you?

In this powerful and deeply personal book, SaBrina Fisher Reece explores the truth about human nature: we are all born into a world of polarity. Light and shadow. Compassion and cruelty. Fear and love. The tension is not proof that you are broken—it is proof that you have been given free will.

This book does not label people as evil. It does not shame anger, frustration, or human imperfection. Instead, it teaches you how to recognize the internal tug-of-war we all experience and how to consciously choose the higher path without denying your humanity.

Through raw personal stories, leadership lessons, parenting moments, business experiences, and spiritual insight, SaBrina reveals how polarity shows up in everyday life-at work, in relationships, in traffic, in conflict, and even in your own thoughts. She demonstrates that self-regulation, compassion, emotional control, and imagination are powerful tools that help you move toward integrity instead of impulse.

You will learn:

How to understand the "dark side" without being ashamed of it

Why emotional control is a life-saving skill

How small daily choices shape your character

The difference between reacting and choosing

How compassion creates a better world without tolerating abuse

Why discipline is required to consistently choose your higher self

This book is for men, women, and young people who want to grow spiritually without judgment or religious condemnation. It is for those who understand that while horrific acts exist in the world, no one is born destined for darkness. We are given a choice every day.

You wake up at the center of the pole.

The direction you lean becomes the person you become.

If you are ready to understand yourself more deeply, lead with your heart, and consciously choose the higher side of who you are, this book will guide you there.

9 781971 622644